Anthropological and Archaeological Research and Development

Anthropological and Archaeological Research and Development

Edited by

Sachindra Narayan

GYAN

GYAN PUBLISHING HOUSE

NEW DELHI-110002

ANTHROPOLOGICAL AND ARCHAEOLOGICAL RESEARCH AND DEVELOPMENT
[*Anthropology and Archaeology*]

ISBN: 81-212-0619-7

Published in 1999 in India by
Gyan Publishing House
5, Ansari Road
New Delhi 110 002

Laser Typeset at Alphabet, Delhi
Printed at Mehra Offset Press, New Delhi.

Contents

List of Maps

Preface

Anthropology, the science of man in its totality, has come a long way from the early days of descriptive ethnography. Recently, we discussed and decided the priorities of Anthropological Research for the man of twenty-first century. The Anthropological tools and techniques need to be reoriented in order to understand the dimensions and perspectives of man of twenty-first century.

The XIII International Congress of Prehistoric and Protohistoric Sciences was held at Forli, Italy during 8th to 14th September, 1996. The participants of this congress were from almost all countries of the world. The scientific session of the congress was organised into Eighteen scientific sessions. Twenty-three workshops, eighteen Poster Sections and twenty-one posters of the workshop.

The ten selected papers printed in this book are the selected papers of the scientific session of the XIII International Congress of Prehistoric and Protohistoric sciences of which I was chairperson. The discussion part of the scientific session of these papers are not included here because I feel that those are not of the general interest. These papers are being published in the interest of the scientific knowledge and also because these are the rare research papers in which the scholars and students of Prehistoric, Archaeology and Anthropology have much interest.

In the statute of the union the words Prehistoric and Protohistoric sciences mean all the discipline such as Archaeology, Anthropology, Geology, Animal and vegetal palaeontology, ethnology, folklore and sociology which contribute to the development of knowledge in the field of Prehistory and Protohistory. This international body was founded on 28th May 1991 as the successor to the Congress Palaeontologique International (1864) and the Congress International Anthropologic et d Archaeologic Prehistorique (1867) on 29th September, 1955 this Congress became a member of the International Council for Philosophy and Humanistic sciences (CIPSH) which is associated with UNESCO. I sincerely thank The Permanent Council of the International Union of Prehistoric Sciences for choosing me to be the chairperson of the scientific session of the XIIIth UISPP and also to the organisers and the scholars who presented their papers in Forli, Italy in September, 1996.

The first paper of this volume traces the Anthropological and Archaeological research and development in India.

In the second paper Guido Barbujani has analysed that how genetics and linguistics are used as tools for reconstructing the past.

In the third paper Giorgio Manzi has mentioned that towards the end of the middle Pleistocene, archaic humanics-living in three continents (Asia, Africa and Europe) and both hemispheres after a long evolutionary history — were subjected to solution pressures which influenced their biology and culture. In condition of geographical isolation population diversified in regional morphetypes which had different histories and destinies. It is from this geographical dispensation and biological variability that emerged the modern human species.

The fourth paper is by Francesco Barone on Cosmic, Cultural and Biological evolutionism.

The fifth paper is of Jens Poulsen on the Bronze Age Barrows in Denmark. Located at the top of the European Continent and surrounded by the sea lies Denmark, just the opposite of Italy which is also surrounded by the sea located below the continent. It is interesting to look at the archaeologies of the country which have specialised in plough agriculture way back in history and prehistory.

The sixth paper is of Luiz O Osterbeek on Teaching and Training archaeology at Tomar in Portugal. The paper presents an outline of the origins, present and foreseen future of archaeology at the E seela de Technologia de Tomar.

The seventh paper is prehistory and history by Giancarlo Susini. If history is regulated by time, it does not seem possible or at least it is arguable — that these could be time outside history. We all know that, in our everyday life time spent in waiting rooms is usually difficult to measure, much so that the moment in which the waiting end is conditioned by the psychosis created by the waiting. When the mind turns to prehistory a large part of public opinion suffers from similar feelings to those felt by a patient in awaiting room: prehistory is almost universally considered as the waiting room of history.

The eighth paper is on Art and Conceptuality of the Homo Sapiens by Emmannuel Anati. It is quite interesting paper on the subject.

The ninth paper is on Anthropology, Proteins and DNA: Molecules as a tool in the reconstruction of human evolution by Giovanni Destro-Bisol. In this paper the author presents a short overview of the use of proteins and DNA as a tool for reconstructing human evolutionary history.

The last paper of this volume is on Human Development and World Peace by S.B. Sahai. It is an interesting paper on the subject.

I am thankful to the administration, typing and library stream of this Institute who always come readily whenever I require any assistance. My wife Mrs. Shobha Narayan deserves special thanks because she always take care of the domestic and household affair thereby allowing me to remain free for academic work. I am thankful to Mr. Amit Garg for publishing this book.

Sachindra Narayan

Vijay Dashmi '98
Patna.

[illegible] present and [illegible] as the [illegible]

The present paper is prehistory and history [illegible] [illegible] that these could be [illegible] [illegible] [illegible]

The [illegible] papers on Art and [illegible] by [illegible] of Assam. It is quite interesting paper on the [illegible]

[illegible] paper on Anthropology [illegible] of [illegible] In this paper, the author [illegible] [illegible] and DNA [illegible] evolutionary history.

[illegible] on Human [illegible] It is an interesting paper on the [illegible]

[illegible] the [illegible]

[illegible]

1

Anthropological and Archaeological Research and Development in India

Sachindra Narayan

Anthropology is the science of man in its totality. Archaeology concerns with the material remains of man's past. The source-materials of archaeology are both things made and used by man. Therefore, anthropologists evince keen interest in archaeology in order to gain a holistic study of man.

One of the major approaches to archaeology originated about the middle of the nineteenth century. It could be called the approach of the social sciences—most characteristically to anthropology. It arose as part of the magnificent burst of activity in the natural sciences of Charles Darwin, T.H. Huxley, etc., stimulated by the thought of such anthropologists as L.H. Morgan and Sir Edward Tylor who reasoned that if there were a process of biological evolution, then there was a process of social evolution also.

Man is a tradition-bound social animal. He learns to do things by being taught by the older generation and therefore tends to reproduce the same material and social forms. Changes in evolution and degeneration occur in all kinds of societies, but in simpler societies with which the archaeologist is generally concerned, are slow and less abrupt than in modern societies, wherein, technological change take place at a rapid rate. Through the paleolithic period, lasting tens of thousands of years, a limited number of forms of stone tools were manufactured by the same technique. With the passage of time since man's emergence from the primitive state as a tool-making and tool-using animal and with the increase in population and consequent growth or elaboration of cultural equipment, the tempo of cultural change has also accelerated. Basic assumptions underlying systematic typology are that cultural change will be evidenced in the material objects and that this change takes place both in terms of space (geographic spread) and time (chronology). By mapping the location of sites and determining the geographic distribution of cultures it is often possible to find correlation of cultural areas with natural environmental areas, to determine settlement patterns and shifts of population centres through time, and by comparing the local or regional sequences to gain insight into cultural and historical processes over wider areas.

Having performed the labour of excavation and the task of classification, it remains for the archaeologist to treat the historical problem of how the culture he is studying came to constitute the particular aggregation of traits which it displays. Such explanations, which are rarely complete and precise, entail reference to what are called "culture processes", the factors operating towards the change, growth or stabilization of cultures. Culture types which are geographically widespread may be assumed to have diffused from one generative centre in the course of time, and the point of origin can often be indicated as the locus where it occurs earliest or in the most complex form. Cultural traits or trait complexes are often observed to have discontinuous distribution. If the spatial discontinuity is very large and diffusion from one source is judged improbable or the temporal placement of the occurrences is markedly different, the archaeologist may conclude that independent or parallel invention explains the multiple occurrences. The cultural parallels occurring on either side of the Pacific have been judged by some anthropologists to indicate trans-Pacific cultural diffusion and by others as explainable in terms of parallel or independent development. Proof of such alternative explanations can rarely be adduced and the decision to support one or the other usually rests upon what the student believes the weight of probability bears most heavily on.

Some cultural-historical facts or situations can be explained with reference to ecological factors so that types of culture are sometimes noted to correspond in their distribution to natural or ecological zones. This was well illustrated by Alfred L. Kroeber in his study of later American-Indian cultures, where types of native culture are shown. Walter W. Jaylor argued that space-time problems are not so important as what he termed the "conjunctive approach" or functional interpretation of archaeological data in which excavation results are written up in the manner of an ethnography of a living culture by identifying the function of each object. The synthesization of pre-history into schemes of evolutionary cultural stages was attempted by V. Gordon Childe and a sequential culture epoch formulation of wide application was advanced by Julian H. Steward.

Anthropology, has been rightly said to be the mirror of man. Indian anthropology owes its origin to the Asiatic Society of Bengal, which was established in 1774 by Sir William Jones to study "nature and man". In the last two hundred and twenty-five years, Indian anthropology has marched ahead and attempts have been made by anthropologists in the past viz., S.C. Roy (1922), S.C. Dube (1966), N.K. Bose (1963), D.N. Majumdar (1950, 1956) and L.P. Vidyarthi (1966, 1968) to classify the course of development in terms of the dominant trends in anthropological investigation. While it was too early for S.C. Roy (1922) to classify the ethnographic studies in terms of time perspective, he simply categorized them in terms of the source of publication, i.e. magazines, handbooks, monographs, etc. He also attempted to identify the nationality of the authors who conducted investigation among different tribes and castes in India. Again, S.C. Dube (1962) and N.K. Bose (1963) also did not make any explicit attempt to categorize the anthropological materials in terms of meaningful historical sequences. However, the attempts of D.N. Majumdar (1956) and L.P. Vidyarthi (1966, 1978), to make scientific classification of different phases of Indian anthropology were quite significant. Borrowing the terms of T.K. Penniman (1935), D.N. Majumdar for the first time divided the anthropological researches in India into three phases viz. formulatory (1774-1911), construction (1912-37) and critical, 1938 onwards).

In the beginning of the formulatory period, however, the establishment of the Asiatic Society of Bengal was the only choice as it marked the beginning of the scientific study of "nature and man" in India. The beginning of the second phase is marked by the publication of the first full-length monograph entitled *Munda and Their Country*, by S.C. Roy. The beginning of the period from 1938, known as the critical period as put forward by Majumdar coincides with the silver jubilee celebrations of the Indian Science Congress when many foreign anthropologists including B.K. Malinowaski came to India and created an atmosphere allowing for critical studies of Indian tribes and castes.

Anthropology has been on the march through the ages. 'The Child of Darwin' as Marret called it, in a way, celebrated its centenary with *The Origin of Species* in 1859. However, it took a considerably long time to get it professionally institutionalized on the global basis when the British anthropologists took the initiative to organize the First International Congress of Anthropological and Ethnological Sciences in London in 1934. By this time, the British evolutionary and diffusionist theories had emerged as the most important school of thought. This formative phase of institutionalization of anthropology further strengthened the British Social Anthropology and created a climate in its favour at the global level. This trend was further strengthened during the Second World Congress held at Copenhagen in 1938. During the Second World War, anthropology, however, became almost dead and needed revitalization.

When the Congress met in Vienna in 1952, with Wilhelm Schmidt, the noted scholar of Austrian School of Diffusion, the 'Science of Man', as it were, was reborn after the ravages of the Second World War. With increased vigour, it covered new areas of research and thus created a climate for consolidation and expansion. The World Congress held in Philadelphia (1956), for the first time in the United States, amply brought to light the post-war dominance of American anthropology. It was marked by participation of scholars drawn from different parts of the world including the delegates from Russia for the first time. The Philadelphia Congress, viewed in the background of the historic International Symposium on Anthropology organized by Wennue-Green Foundation for Anthropological Research at New York in 1952 under the chairmanship of A.L. Kroeber, accelerated support to the American model of anthropology. In his introductory remarks, Kroeber observes emphatically: After all, the subject of anthropology is limited only by man. It is not restricted by time, it goes back into geology as far as man can be traced. It is not restricted by region but it is worldwide in its scope. It has specialized on the primitive man because no other science would deal seriously with them, it has never renounced its intent to understand the higher civilization also (A.L. Kroeber: 1953: xiii).

The American model of anthropology decidedly found all-round recognition in the symposium and, among many. Levi-Strauss agreed that "Anthropology has a close relationship with humanities, social sciences and natural sciences". He further observed that "Anthropology tries to jump to a deep level, while social sciences have been, so far, unable to do so, and the result is an extremely difficult situation for cooperation between anthropology and the social sciences".

Margaret Mead further classified Levi-Strauss's stand and amplified his statement. She observed: "Anthropology uses methods of analysis from different levels with different units and different time-scales, cross-cutting all disciplines relating from man to nature on the one hand and history on the other hand".

The integrated image of anthropology, which emerged from the 1952 symposium and its approaches for studying the 'integrated' man, was further followed up in the planning and deliberation of the Fifth International Congress of Anthropological and Ethnological Sciences (1956) in the publication of current anthropology. American anthropology further enriched itself by initiating the publication of *Current Anthropology* edited by Soltax since 1960. It carried the spirit of integration further in anthropology as it continued to publish papers from all over the world on pre-history, archaeology, linguistics, folklore, ethnology, social anthropology and physical anthropology.

Later on, the International Congress of Anthropological and Ethnological Sciences, held in New Delhi, 1978, Vancouver, 1983, Zagreb, 1988, and Mexico, 1988, had a separate and important symposium on pre-history and archaeology. Development in global anthropology cannot be understood in the holistic perspective without understanding the role of pre-historical and archaeological researches. So is the case also with the development of Indian anthropology.

Anthropological and archaeological researches in India have made positive contribution into the growth of the knowledge of the discipline and more so in the general development of the population of the country. It has made a significant contribution in preserving, maintaining and transmitting the heritage of India to the 21st century.

REFERENCES

Addison, Wesley, 1972, *Current Topics in Anthropology*, Vol. I, Modular Publications.

Bhowmik, K.L., 1988, *Current Anthropological and Archaeological Perspectives*, Inter-India Publications, New Delhi.

Clark, Grahame and Piggott, Stuart, 1965, *Pre-historic Societies*, Penguin Books, Harmondsworth, U.K.

Kroeber, A.L., 1957, *Anthropology Today*, Chicago Press, Chicago.

Narayan, S., 1988, *Indian Anthropology*, Gyan Publishing House, New Delhi.

———, 1988, *Social Anthropology*, Gyan Publishing House, New Delhi.

———, 1994, *Strategies for World Peace*, Common Wealth Publications, New Delhi.

Roy, S.C., 1972, *Oraon Religion and Custom*, Editions Indian, Calcutta.

Vidyarthi, L.P., 1979, *Rise of World Anthropology*, Concept Publications, New Delhi.

2

Genetics and Linguistics as Tools for Reconstructing the Past

Guido Barbujani

Humankind has been on the earth for many thousands of years. Most anthropologists and geneticists believe that our first ancestors existed around 1,50,000 years ago.[1] By "our first ancestors" we mean individuals similar to us in appearance, who are technically defined as "anatomically modern men". Others consider longer ranges of time, which extend up to 800,000 years ago. We know very little about this long lapse of time which we shall in a rather less than rigorous way, call the history of humanity even if it would be more correct to speak of pre-history. We have written evidence only about the last phase, some thousands of years and this too, not for all geographical areas. Besides this, it is only the clues supplied to us by archaeology and palaeontology which permit us to satisfy certain curiosities about the life of our predecessors. The greater part of our past is substantially unknown to us.

In the last ten or fifteen years, however, two apparently distant academic disciplines have also begun to tell us something about the most remote periods of human history; these being linguistics and genetic. Their relationship with the study of the past would seem to come down to the fact that however one looks at it; the history of humanity is one single entity. Archaeologists, linguists and geneticists work with different data, but all the characteristics of human population, from the form of their utensils to their lexis and to their genes have been determined in the course of the same historical development.

Over the centuries technologies have become more complex, languages, more numerous, and in some cases simple, and genes have undergone mutations and variations of frequency; but, in the final analysis, all of these changes have affected the same people and the same population. For this reason, languages, genes and archaeological find, in practice every human characteristic, should preserve traces of the same sequence of events, and, if interpreted correctly should give us coherent information about it. Beyond this principle, however, methodological differences have, for a long time, rendered comparisons between results obtained in various fields difficult or near impossible.

What has happened recently is that geneticists and linguists have realized that they have something additional in common. First of all, their data are similar, i.e. a population to study in some point on the earth, its characteristics linguistics or genetic, and the characteristics of its neighbour in order to make comparison. It was, in effect, the spread of the comparative method which brought to light the fact that the differences between peoples are not random; both the differences in the genes which their members carry and transmit, and the differences in the languages which they speak and teach their children. We are not talking about a genuine discovery, but rather the systematization of already existing knowledge. Archaeologists have known for quite some time that neighbouring peoples (in time and space) tend to become similar to one another[2] and they base their deductions on these resemblances. In the same way they have come to understand that languages and genes often differ according to the distances between the populations in space and time. There are exceptions, but certain regularities are evident. It is well known, for example, that Italian includes various dialects, and has points of contact with French and Sardo (its neighbours) and with Latin (its ancestor). Linguistic identity suggests that two populations descend from the same recent ancestor, and linguistic similarity that they come from the same ancestor in the same way, but further back in time.[3] The same analysis can be made from genetic variants or alleles present in populations which occur in similar forms, and with similar frequency in neighbouring peoples (between which migration is easy) or in peoples which are interrelated (which might not be contiguous today but have common origins we can think of the African populations, for example, and the blacks shipped to the America in the age of the slave trade). Thus, archaeological, linguistic and genetic data show characteristic progressions, or patterns.

A convergence between fields of study which are so diverse would not have been possible without the development of similar methods for the analysis of data. Among the many possible examples in both fields, relations between populations are often represented in the form of trees. Representation as a tree presupposes that an ancestral entity (a population of which the language or genes interest us) be subdivided into independent entities which in their turn are further subdivided and so on. There are certain snags, the main one being that in this way the effects of geographical distance and of secondary contacts after subdivision are disregarded; effects which, as we shall see, cannot be irrelevant at all. The important thing is, however, that in this way, it becomes possible to compare the results of the genetic and linguistic analyses, both with each other and with archaeological model. From the basis of these various archaeological, linguistic and genetic data, chronologies of the population splits can be defined; each chronology is obtained in an independent manner, but then is comparable with the others. Relations among the three sciences are more subtle and complex than this, and have also permitted sophisticated analyses in the last decade. Nevertheless, the use of model trees seems, to me, to be a good example. The assumptions necessary to construct a language tree are not the same as those used in genetics, nor in archaeology and the level of precision in dating is also different. The fact remains, that thanks to trees and other modern methods of analysis, researchers from various academic backgrounds have found a common language. In conclusion, it is possible to reconstruct historical events based upon the patterns of linguistic and genetic diversity.

Reconstructions based on genetic or linguistic patterns do not have, of themselves, a greater value than traditional ones, based on archaeological evidence. What is important is exactly the opportunity to compare hypothesis based on different, and independent data. It is easy to be mistaken and may always happen that apparent relationships between various utensils, or between a group of languages, do not correspond on the level of the historic relationship between the peoples who used those utensils or spoke those languages. But it is unlikely that archaeological, linguistic and genetic data be consistent with each other, and, at the same time, all wrong. If various data suggest the same relationships among populations, it is very probable that these relationships reflect a unique chain of historical events, namely the one that actually occurred.

In the following paragraphs the points of contact between linguistics and genetics can be seen more clearly. Some technical details will be necessary, but to an indispensable minimum. We shall then go on to discuss briefly theories about the evolution of languages and genes. I would like to point out, from the outset, that the term "evolution" is not popular with linguistics: nevertheless, once it is made clear that it is not a synonym for "progress". I do not see why it should not be used, in a similar way to practice in biology.

Evolutionary Trees as a Means to Summarize the Past

Let us assume that we are dealing with different data sets: different languages, or data about certain genes in different populations. The fundamental question in both cases is essentially the same: how is it that things are as they are, and not different? A good way of beginning to answer this is to obtain a classification. At first, languages or genes can be compared pairwise. One may ask how many words of the various pairs of languages are different, and to what extent do they differ. Alternatively, the differences between various alleles or between their frequencies, can be considered, once again pairwise, comparing populations. In this case we are talking about the calculation of linguistic and genetic distances. Sometimes this is enough for us to understand something about our past. The white populations of the British Isles and Australia are close, linguistically and genetically, notwithstanding the great geographical distance between them. Even if the memory of the migrations from Europe to Oceania during the last three centuries were lost, this information would be enough to demonstrate that the two populations are related. If, however, the number of populations considered increase, this first step is not sufficient. The population 'A' will differ substantially at the linguistic or genetic level, from 'B', 'C' and 'D' but will be similar to 'E', 'F' and 'G' and so on for all the others. It is difficult to memorize so many relationships, and even more difficult to interpret them. Thus, the next step is to look for a synthesis. As I said earlier, very often one tries to visualize the levels of resemblance in the form of a tree. Trees of this type, or "dendrograms", summarize what we defined earlier as patterns of genetic or linguistic similarity. The number of words by which two languages differ, or the genetic differences, are proportional to the length of the branches which join them. Similarly, populations are connected by short branches, dissimilar ones by long branches.

Strictly speaking, a tree does not tell us when or where these variations had their origin. But the simplest interpretation is to say that large differences are accumulated in long periods of separation and small differences indicate a common recent origin of the languages or genes of the two groups. The deeper separations of the tree would thus depend upon older phenomena of differentiation and the smaller branches on more recent phenomena. It is important to note that in this way a particular significance is attributed to the branching points of the tree. Each of these nodes might correspond to a primitive form of a language often not documented or to a collection of genes in a population about which in general nothing is known. With this step, however, the tree becomes something different, and more interesting. It is no longer a simple representation of the levels of relatedness between populations but it has become the outline of an historical process. We have moved from description to interpretation.

Let us see how the passage from the descriptive tree to its analysis in evolutionary terms is justified, keeping in mind the fact that some degree of arbitrariness is inevitable in any models. On the linguistic level we know that present languages developed through phases corresponding to languages which are now extinct. Italian and French, which have numerous words and grammatical structures, in common, come from one same ancestor (Latin); both have an ancestor in common but more distant, (probably some form of Proto-Indo-European) with languages like English, Armenian, Persian (Farsi) and Hindi, which are quite similar to one another, but not to the extent of Italian and French. If this is true, one can assume that the resemblance between languages whose ancestor is not known depends on a completely analogous process of divergence; the greater the time elapsed since then, the greater the difference. The same reasoning is applied to genetic relationships. In both cases we turn to two fundamental postulates:

1. Genetic and linguistic diversity is accumulated by way of a series of splits between populations, represented in the tree by bifurcations;
2. Levels of diversity are approximately proportional to the time elapsed since separation. In other words, present linguistic and genetic variations are essentially regarded as the result of demographic phenomena of the past.

Linguistic Change and Biological Evolution

Is it really like that? How sure are we that languages and genes diversified during the same demographic processes, with a gradual increase of differences between groups? Is it legitimate to neglect the contacts these groups will have, certainly had, even after they were separated from one another? And how important is that geographically close populations generally have more intense exchanges, both at the biological and the cultural level? It is not possible to give an overall answer. We can, however, consider how languages and genes evolve and reformulate the question on the basis of what we know and whether it is reasonable to think that trees of linguistic and genetic resemblance summarize the history of populations with acceptable accuracy?

In the world there are more than 5000 languages.[4] Many of these are spoken by very few individuals, especially in Australia and the Americas, and seem to be destined to disappear very quickly. The number of languages actually depends on the definition of language and dialect, about which not all linguists agree. Whatever their status, however, these languages or dialects reveal resemblances and differences; which is to say, family relationships. The first family to be identified was the Indo-

European, followed quickly by others. William Jones was the first one, in the seventeenth century, to note the similarities among Sanskrit, Ancient Greek, Latin and other languages.[5] The verb "to bear", for example, in the three persons singular of the present is *bharami, bharasi, bharati* in Sanskrit *phero, phereis, pherei* in Greek, *fero, fers, fert* in Latin and "I bear, you bear, he bears" in modern English. The resemblance is obvious, even at the level of grammatical elements (the inflexion in 's' of the second person, for example, which occurs in three out of four cases). Jones deduced that all of these languages have a common origin. Given, that many European languages derive from Latin or Greek, and many Indian languages from Sanskrit, it becomes clear that a good proportion of Europeans and Asians speak languages related to one another.

Other linguistic families have been put forward but not all of them have been accepted with the same degree of certainty by the majority of experts. If we leave out the details, however, a surprisingly simple picture emerges. Only 17 linguistic families may exist, in addition to very few linguistic isolates the most famous of which is Basque. By definition, all the languages in a family are connected by genealogical relationships, i.e., they come from the same ancestral language. Not much is known about linguistic relationships on a large-scale, but some linguists maintain that there are common elements to be found in various families, which would thus form macro-families. One of the most important, to which we shall come back later, is called the Nostratic macro-family, and includes at least five families, among these the Indo-European. Certain lexical and grammatical elements might indeed be present in all the languages in the world, which would testify to a common origin for all of them. We are dealing with theories as yet unproven; certainly there are a lot of languages, but it is possible to put them together into a relatively small number of groups, each with a common origin. The formal resemblance between this structuring of linguistic diversity and its representation in the form of a tree is quite clear. But it is possible to go further.

How is it that things are like this? The British archaeologist, Colin Renfrew, has identified four fundamental mechanisms by which languages have reached their present geographical distribution.[6] For the purpose of this study it is unnecessary to establish whether Renfrew's classification is completely exhaustive, or if it needs to be modified. Instead we need to see if the mechanisms postulated are consistent with the idea that languages evolve mainly owing to demographic processes that first the populations separate, then their languages diverge. No one believes that this is the only possible form of linguistic change, but it is sufficient that this is the principle mechanism for interaction with genetics to be productive. If instead it were demonstrated that the phenomena of contamination and mixing are prevalent a representation in the form of a tree would clearly be unsuitable.

According to Renfrew, languages spread by colonization, substitution, divergence and convergence. By colonization is meant, that a population expands into a previously uninhabited territory, that takes its own language there. Substitution is the process whereby a group loses its linguistic identity, taking on that of another group. Divergence is the phenomenon where two groups which speak the same language separate, and as a result, the linguistic novelties which come about in either one do not spread to the other; the opposite process of convergence is seen as a result of contacts. If we think again of the representation of history in the form of a tree, it is clear that the (demographic) process of separation of population prompts divergence, at the linguistic level although colonization can come about in a successive phase. Colonization and divergence for this reason seem to determine a pattern of linguistic diversity analogous at that which can be represented in the form of a dendrogram. It remains to be seen whether these mechanisms play a greater role than substitution and convergence, which shall be discussed later.

As far as biological evolution is concerned, models of separation and divergence have been used for thirty years now,[7] and have reached a high level of formalization. In general, separation between groups is followed by an increasing isolation and as a consequence the new alleles introduced by mutation do not spread from one group to another. The frequencies of the alleles present in each group vary independently, and on an average they tend to diverge. In many cases it is seen that the genetic differences between groups of which the times of separation are known are indeed proportional to the times of reciprocal isolation. As with languages, populations exist whose differences cannot be explained so easily, and as for languages, it often depends on contacts between populations, and in particular, on the intensity of their migratory exchanges. Thus, the reconstruction of history in the form of a tree is also plausible for genes on the condition that the phenomena of divergence and isolation have prevailed over those which pull in the opposite direction, i.e. migration and intermixing.

What History do Genes tell us, and what do Languages tell us?

In a nutshell, if linguistic and genetic divergence are mainly the result of demographic phenomena of separation, language trees and gene trees should resemble one another and should lead to consistent inferences. If, on the other hand, phenomena of convergence and intermixing were important in the history of certain people, or of all of them, the results of genetic and linguistic studies should be contradictory. In 1988 Robert Sokar[8] demonstrated that there is a close correlation between genetic linguistic and geographical distances between European populations. Genetic distances correlate above all with geographical distances; which is to say that the closed biological relationships seem to be those between groups living in geographically close localities. But when, with appropriate statistical procedures, we eliminate the effect of correlation with geography, linguistic distances also result as correlating to genetic distances. Sokal draws two conclusions from this. The first is that the effect of geography is not to be neglected—if neighbouring populations tend to resemble one another it is because they exchange more genes than distant populations do—and this indicates that phenomena of convergence exist, and, are important. The second conclusion is that, however, a correlation also exists between languages and genes, and it survives notwithstanding the phenomena of convergence which we have just spoken about.[9]

Thus, a model in which demographic events of separation determine genetic and linguistic differences in parallel is reasonable on the whole. A confirmation of these results exists in the fact that, not only in Europe, but also in other continents, the boundaries between different languages are often areas in which genetic differences are also strong. Thus similar languages tend to be spoken by peoples who have similar genes, and different languages are accompanied by significant genetic differences.[10] There are exceptions but the rule seems to be this.

A demonstration that the parallel evolution of genes and languages leads to congruent trees was given in 1988, by Luca Cavalli-Sforza's group.[11] The tree put together by comparing the frequencies of 120 genetic variants in 42 populations from all over the world contains groupings which are very similar to those which can be predicted on the basis of linguistic affinities. Even if some details have not been clarified if, for example, the fundamental split at the genetic and linguistic level is really between Africans and non-Africans or whether the European populations are close to the Africans,[12] a substantial consistency between gene-trees and language-trees seems to be well supported by data. This consistency is not to be taken for granted, but to be verified with each new case that we are facing. Certainly peoples exist whose language has evolved via processes independent from those which have determined their genetic characteristics. Clear examples are the Uralic languages in Europe (above all Hungarians, but also Finnish[13] and the languages of the European colonials in Africa, Australia, Asia and the Americas, (Spanish, Portuguese, English and French). In all of these cases a relatively small group assumed a dominant position in society and imposed its own language. This drastic linguistic change however was not accompanied by an equally significant change in the composition of the population, and therefore of its genetic characteristics. There are also examples of genetic change in a substantial linguistic continuity, here a thought can be given to the composition of the population of the United States in the last century. Overall, however, it really seems that the history of many peoples can be represented as a series of processes of separation which have left recognizable traces at the linguistic and genetic levels.

Once it is accepted that it is legitimate to use genetic data to understand linguistic variation, and vice versa, the only problem is to choose among many interesting issues. The open questions are numerous. Up to now it has been possible to give an answer to only a few of them; but sometimes the results have exceeded the expectations. The study of the indigenous peoples of the Americas is an example in which genetic data have been useful for resolving linguistic queries. Later on we shall see, on the other hand, an example of the use of linguistic information in genetic analysis, while speaking about the diffusion of agriculture in Eurasia.

How Many Migrations to the Americas?

Until the last decade our understanding of the linguistic diversity in the Americas was not satisfactory. Even though it was the second-last continent to be colonized by Man (just before Oceania). America seemed to contain a number of languages and a linguistic diversity superior to that of any other continent. According to some experts there were up to some 200 independent families of languages (compared to 14 in the rest of the world). Even Africa, where human presence has been documented for a period five or ten times as long, seemed to be much more homogeneous on the linguistic level. Nevertheless, it is quite well established that the number of languages present in a region depends, at least as a rough approximation, on the time which the peoples have had to diversify. The American linguist Joseph Greenberg, has put forward a proposal of radical simplification: the differences between almost all the American languages are evident but superficial: their common elements suggest to attribute them to a single, vast family which Greenberg suggests calling "Amerind".[14] Besides the Amerind, there might be only two other families of languages in the America—the Eskimo-Aleut and the Na-Dene, present in small groups in Canada and the United States.

It is not useful to enter here into a discussion of the value of the linguistic evidence in favour of, or against Greenberg's theory. Among others, Douglas Wallace's and Svante Paabo's groups have looked for confirmation of it on the genetic level. Translated into demographic terms, Greenberg's proposal is more or less like this—the three American families of languages might correspond to separate groups which arrived in America in distinct waves. To make this open to verification it is enough to imagine that each wave was characterized by specific genes, and thus is, at least in principle, distinguishable from the others. Obviously, if we meet a strong genetic difference between single populations attributed by Greenberg to the same family (Amerind), it would then be difficult to think of this as the product of the migration of a single Asiatic group, which has since diversified, once established in the new continent.

Wallace and his collaborators have worked on one particular segment of DNA, not present in the nucleus of cells, but in a sub-cellular organism the mitochondrion. This is a region of the genome which is very informative and largely unaffected by biological processes, which, in contrast, complicate the interpretation of the analysis of other areas of DNA. The study of some hundreds of individuals of different languages, from America and Asia, has given strong support to Greenberg's hypothesis. Essentially there are only four types of DNA (mt DNA) (or rather four groups of similar types) in the mitochondria of the native Americans. These four types are present in various proportions in the various populations of Amerindian languages, but only two of them are present in the Na-Dene (it has not yet been possible to characterize people of Eskimo-Aleuti language). Not only this, each mt DNA has been found in low frequency in the peoples of north-east Asia and Siberia, which indicates a probable origin of the first Americans. Lastly, in representing genetic differences in the form of a tree we arrive at an approximate dating of the origin of the Amerindian and Na-Dene groups, viz. around 20,000 and less than 10,000 years ago respectively, which is in complete agreement with the paleontological data. This work demonstrates it seems to me, how the comparison between linguistic and genetic evidence allows previously impossible syntheses. The picture that emerges is one in which one or a few migrations occurred of individuals of Asiatic origin into the American continent, and certainly not two hundred. The oldest migration allowed the spread of a population which extended as far as Tierra del Fuego in about 20,000 years, fragmenting and differentiating linguistically and genetically, but, which contained only a small number of different genes. Its lack of genetic variation leads us to understand that we are dealing with the migration of few individuals, from which all the present-day people descend. The peoples of the Na-Dene language are seen as the fruit of a more recent migration, the similarity between their mt DNA and that of the Amerindians could indicate an origin from the same Asiatic region, or (less probably) could be due to a recent partial inter-mixing.[15]

Who were the First Indo-Europeans?

For obvious reasons, Europe is the part of the world which has been described with the greatest precision, both from the linguistic and genetic point of view. It is no coincidence then that the first comparison of genetic data on a large-scale was done on European populations, and that this study (by Paolo Menozzi, Alberto Piazza and Luca Cavalli-Sforza)[16] marked the beginning of a period in which genetics has tried to go beyond the description of the structure of populations, to define the sequence of events which populations have passed through.

In this first study it was shown that the frequencies of many genetic variants are distributed in a systematic way spatially for in Europe the main genetic characteristics is the presence of wide gradients. Many alleles have their maximum frequency in the Near East and then become rarer and rarer as one moves west or north. Such a pattern could not be due to change, as has indeed been shown. The explanation put forward in 1978 and confirmed by successive studies[17] is that its origin is in the spread of the first Neolithic farmers. From about 10,000 years ago indeed, there appear traces of agricultural activity (tools and fossil seeds) first in an area of Anatolia and the Near East, and then more and more towards the West and North, reaching as far as the Iberian Peninsula and the British Isles around 3000 BC. Basically the spread of agricultural technologies could have taken place mainly by cultural transmission, or because the individuals practising agriculture moved, i.e. via population dispersal. There is no way to resolve this alternative from the archaeological point of view, but the genetic consequences of the two processes are very different

In the first case, with the hypothesis that agricultural practices were transmitted culturally, we do not expect any particular distribution of genetic variants. If however, some people who practised agriculture expanded, thus introducing its own technologies into new areas, then the characteristic genes of this population would also have spread. Gradients of gene frequencies are for this reason only predicted by the model of demic spread; and seeing as these have been observed it is logical to conclude, that farmers, rather than farming, spread. It is believed in particular that population growth caused by greater availability of food determined the necessity to cultivate ever greater areas. Thus, the expansion of the first Neolithic farmers should have occurred through gradual widening of their territories, and should not have required true migrations.

The details of the model are not insignificant, and have been the subject of progressive adjustments. Especially it has been shown that continental gradients can be determined only under two conditions, one, if the expanding population continues to grow during the expansion, and two, if there is little, or effectively no mixing with peoples encountered during the expansion.

This process is indicated by the term "demic diffusion". One cannot exclude the possibility that in certain areas agricultural activities had a different origin, and could have been introduced by cultural means. But there is no way of explaining the genetic gradients observed, if not by thinking that the prevalent phenomenon was a demographic expansion, accompanied by limited mixing, or even by the substantial elimination of the original peoples which did not practise agriculture.[18] The presence of very accurate archaeological data also suggests a date for expansion which the genetic data document.

Up to now we have not talked about languages. It is sufficient, however, merely to look at a map to realize that Europe is structured not only genetically, as we have just seen, but also linguistically. With a few exceptions, the Europeans speak languages of the same family: Indo-European. Until a few years ago the prevailing opinion among linguistics experts, based, it seems to me, on disputable evidence, was that the first Indo-Europeans had spread from the Steppes to the north of the Caucasus, between the Black Sea and the Caspian Sea, something like 5000 years ago. It was Colin Renfrew who was the first to think that two processes of diffusion, one for agriculture and the other for languages, both coming from the East, could be one too many. In a study dated 1987, and in a series of later articles, in which archaeological sources and genetic data were combined.[19] Renfrew put forward the idea that the Indo-European languages were spoken in the regions where farming had its origins, and were transmitted to Europe by the first farmers, which is much earlier than was generally believed. A single population diffusion could have propagated farming techniques (archaeologically documented), languages and obviously the genes of the Neolithic peoples of the Near East. Renfrew has also indicated how other waves from the same place of origin could have brought agriculture towards the east and south-west, to North Africa and to much of Asia. The idea of this multi-directional spread comes in part from archaeological studies for it looks as if cereals already cultivated around 8000 B.C. were diffused in a roughly centrifugal way, from larger areas than was once thought. But strong support for this idea comes above all from linguistic data which in the same regions of the Near East there were once four families in contact. Altaic (including today various Mongolian languages, Turkish, Korean and Japanese), Elamo-Dravidic (including the languages of South India, among them Telugu and Tamil, and which originally spread as far as present-day Iran) and Afro-Asiatic (including the Berber languages, Arabic and Hebrew), in addition of course to Indo-European, the four families which, according to certain Russian linguists might make up part of the macro-family "Nostratic" and thus might be related to each other.

Schematically then, some linguists have postulated the existence of links between four families of languages which were in geographical contact, even if today they are not and the point of contact corresponds to the region from where on the basis of completely independent archaeological evidence, a multi-directional spread of agricultural technology is imagined to have started. We are dealing, it is clear with a model open to verification on the basis of genetic data. Without entering into the often complex methods employed, we can say that three of these families (Indo-European, Elamo-Dravidic and Altaic) show clear gradients of gene frequencies, matching those found by Cavalli-Sforza's group in its study of Europe. Afro-Asiatic is an exception for which the results are contradictory, but not explicitly against the expectations of the Renfrew model. It is very difficult to explain genetic similarities on such a vast scale, from Portugal to Central Asia, if it is not accepted that they were determined in the course of a huge process of demographic expansion. Phenomena of this magnitude certainly did not occur after the Neolithic period, when peoples were tied to their territories by agricultural practices. For this reason it seems probable that we should anticipate the entry of Indo-European languages into Europe to around 10,000 years ago. It also seems that these languages were spread in a completely analogous way to that causing the diffusion of two or three other families of languages which embrace a huge slice of the old world. Thus it is likely that the languages of Europe and Asia spread because the populations which spoke them spread,[20] that is, those who developed the practice of farming first. It is worth stressing that the genetic gradients just described will pass unobserved if the genetic data in each family of languages are not analysed separately.

Conclusion

It is shown how the last ten years have seen a convergence between apparently distant fields of research. The potential of this convergence has been explored only to a limited extent as yet. However, it is already clear that interdisciplinary studies in which linguistic, genetic and archaeological data are compared can tell us much about our prehistory. A satisfactory synthesis of the three disciplines is still a long way off. Linguists must reach a precise classification of the languages of the world, in particular, the relationships between the families of languages recognized today have not been studied much, and the strength of these relationships once it is admitted that they exist, is still to be defined. As regards archaeologists there is a need in part to produce new data in the regions of the world about which knowledge is scarce. The fundamental problem seems to be, however, the step from studying remains to creating models and hypotheses susceptible to verification on the genetic level. An area of particular interest is that related to the contacts between peoples. The presence of similar artefacts in distant populations has traditionally been seen as a proof of migration, but by now it has been shown that this interpretation is unwarranted, and in many cases it is easier to think of commercial contacts. This is a field of research in which an attempt at a re-evaluation of knowledge and of the criteria of interpretation seems to be necessary.

Lastly, taking into account genetics, the large quantity of data produced in recent times carries the danger of obscuring, by the sheer enthusiasm it has generated, the existence of several unresolved problems. In fact, many of the models used in population genetics are based on postulates that are difficult to verify concretely. Extraction of DNA from fossil finds opens fascinating perspectives,[21] but this possibility also carries new ambiguities and problems, the most serious of which is that of contamination, which is to say, to end up characterizing, as has already happened not the DNA of the samples, but of the researcher. It is worth mentioning, a problem which could result in a new separation of the study of genes and of languages. As is well known in the last few years rapid technical advances have allowed geneticists to study DNA directly and not deduce its characteristics by the analysis of proteins. Studies of DNA are necessarily based on relatively small samples (some few tens of individuals), which are however, characterized in a very detailed way. Thus the analysis of the frequencies of various alleles has been mostly abandoned in order to concentrate on their differences at the level of DNA, i.e. on their sequences. Undoubtedly this represents a step forward. The other side of the coin, however, is that the sequences are much more stable in evolutionary terms, than the frequencies of alleles. An allele frequency can change every generation, if the population is small enough, whereas changes in sequences (mutations) come about at a rate of one every few thousand years (with some variation depending on the region of the genome concerned). Now, linguistics experts only accept with reluctance the idea of going beyond 5,000 years ago in their reconstructions. Many believe that more ancient linguistic relationships are practically impossible to recognize. It may be that this is not true, and that even very ancient relationships between languages can be identified, with methods which are at the moment unavailable. And it may be that in the future, genes will be identified which mutate more quickly than those studied up to now, and that in this way the time scale of genetic studies gets shorter again. But in the last few years, indeed, the development of genetic methodologies has brought us to study ever more ancient phenomena, far beyond the temporal limits of linguistics. Thus, it is not clear how long the interaction between linguists and geneticists will continue to be fruitful—perhaps their interests are doomed to diversify again. Before arriving at this sad divorce, however, the marriage between genetics and linguistics still has much to offer.

REFERENCES

1. The most respected estimates of the date of the origin of modern humans are based on paleontological finds; see C.B. Stringer and P. Andrews (1988), Genetic and Fossil Evidence for the Origin of Modern Humans, *Science* 239: 1263-68. Datings based on genetic studies agree in indicating a genesis around 1,50,000 years ago. I. Vigilant, M. Stoneking, H. Harpending, K. Hawkes and A.C. Wilson (1991). African Populations and the Evolution of Human Mitochondrial DNA. *Science*, 253:1503-1507; S. Horai, K. Hayasaka, R. Kondo, K. Tsugane and N. Takahata (1995), "Recent African Origin of Modern Humans Revealed by Complete Sequences of Hominoid Mitochondrial DNA". Proceedings of the National Academy of Sciences USA 92:532-36: and D.B. Goldstein, A. Ruiz Linares, L.L. Cavalli-Sforza and M.W. Feldman (1995) "Genetic and Absolute Dating based on Microsatellites and the Origin of Modern Humans", *Proceedings of the National Academy of Sciences*, USA 92:6723-6727. Recently, however, doubts have been raised regarding these estimates, and it has been suggested to put them back to 400,000 or even 800,000 years ago: C. Willis (1995) "When did Eve Live? An evolutionary Detective Story" *Evolution* 49:593-607.
2. For a description of what has been called the process approach to archaeology, see the work of Renfrew and especially *Archaeology and Languages: The Puzzle of Indo-European Origins*, London: Penguin, 1989.
3. R.R. Sokal (1988) "Genetic, geographic, and linguistic distances in Europe", *Proceedings of the National Academy of Sciences*, USA 88:1722-1726.
4. The most recent classification is in M. Ruhlen, *A Guide to the World's Languages, Vol. I: Classification*, London: Edward Arnold, 1991.
5. C. Renfrew, op. cit., pp. 9-71.

6. C. Renfrew (1989) Models of Change in Language and Archaeology Transactions of the Philological Society 87:103-155.
7. The classic studies in human genetics are by L.I. Cavalli Sforza (1966) "Population Structure and Human Evolution". Proceedings of the Royal Society, 164:362-379, and L.L. Cavalli Sforza and A.J.F. Edwards (1967) Phylogenetic Analysis. Models and Estimation Procedures 19:233-257. A more recent synthesis is by E.M. Wijsman and L.L. Cavalli Sforza (1984) Migration and Genetic Population Structure with Special Reference to Humans. Annual Review of Ecology Systematics, 15:279-301. For a critique of these models, or of their excessive use, see A. Langaney, D. Roessli, N.H. Van Blyenburgh and P. Dard (1992). Do most human populations descend from evolutionary trees? *Human Evolution* 7:47-61.
8. R.R. Sokal (1988), *op. cit.*
9. More exactly, one thinks in this way a demographic event of separation between peoples causes an isolation which has analogous effects at the genetic and linguistic level. In both cases the genetic and linguistic novelties which appear in one group do not tend to spread to the other as well. If these novelties appear at a rate which is, roughly, constant in time as it is reasonable to imagine, the genetic and linguistic differences between the two populations permit us to estimate even if only approximately, times of separation. If instead the two different populations mix there is no reason to believe that the consequent cultural convergence must take place in parallel with the genetic homogenization. Examples abound. Small groups of colonizers (Mongols in Turkey and Hungary, Europeans in Africa and America, Russians in the Caucuses, etc.) imposed their language without substantial genetic changes; black slaves imported to the America rapidly assumed the local language but intermixing with the resident population only to a minimum extent. If a correlation exists between genetic and linguistic differences, this type of phenomena should reduce or annul it.
10. No one believes that different genes determine the capacity to speak different language. If anything, the opposite is true. In many parts of the world linguistic differences slow down exchanges between peoples and prevent these exchanges from cancelling out genetic differences. Comparisons between the distribution of language borders and of areas of strong genetic variability are in G. Barbujani and R.R. Sokal (1990) "Zones of Abrupt Genetic Change in Europe are also Linguistic Boundaries", *Proceedings of the National Academy of Sciences* USA 87:1816-1819; G.Barbujani and R.R. Sokal (1991) Genetic population structure of Italy. II Physical and Cultural

Barriers to Gene Flow, *American Journal of Human Genetics* 48:398-411: L. Excoffier, R.M. Harding, R.R. Sokal, B. Pellegrini and A. Sanchez-Mazas (1991) Spatial differentiation of Rh and Gm Haplotype Frequencies in sub-Saharan Africa and its relation to Linguistic Affinities, *Human Biology* 63:273-307; and G. Barbujani, I.S. Nasidze and G.N. Whitehead (1994) Genetic Diversity in the Caucasus *Human Biology* 66:639-68. For a general discussion of the assumptions and the implications of these studies, see G. Barbujani (1991) What do Languages tell us about Human Micro-evolution. *Trends in Ecology and Evolution* 6:151-155.

11. L.L. Cavalli-Sforza, A. Piazza, P. Menozzi and J. Mountain (1988) "Reconstruction of Human Evolution: Bringing together Genetic, Archaeological and Linguistic Data", *Proceedings of the National Academy of Sciences*, USA 85:6002-6006.
12. The indication that African populations are the most genetically diversified, both internally and with respect to non-Africans comes from many studies, among which, L. Vigilant, M. Stoneking, H. Hawkes and A.C. Wilson (1991) *op. cit.* Indications of a close relationship between Europe and Africa are in A.M. Bowcock and others (1991) "Drift, Admixture and Selection in Human Evolution. A study with DNA Polymorphisms", *Proceedings of the National Academy of Sciences*, USA 88:6723-6727, and in J. Chen, R.R. Sokal and M. Ruhlen (1995) "Worldwide Analysis of Genetic and Linguistic Relationships of Human Populations", *Human Biology* 67:595-612.
13. A. Sajantila and others (1995) "Genes and Languages in Europe: An Analysis of Mitochondrial Lineage", *Genome Research* 5:42-52.
14. The presence of very numerous families of languages in the America has been recently sustained by L. Campbell and M. Mithin (1979). "The Languages of Native America", Austin, Texas, University of Texas Press. The fundamental text is by J.H. Greenberg in 1987. *Language in the Americas*, Stanford, California, Stanford University Press.
15. D.C. Wallace, K. Garrison and W.C. Knowler (1985) "Dramatic Founder Effects in Amerindian Mitochondrial DNAs". *American Journal of Physical Anthropology* 68:149-155; A. Torroni and others (1992) "Native American Mitochondrial DNA analysis indicates that the Amerind and the Nadene populations were founded by two independent migrations", *Genetics* 130:153-162; D.C. Wallace and A. Torroni (1992) "American Indian pre-history as written in the Mitochondrial DNA: A review", *Human Biology* 64:403-416; R.H. Ward, A. Redd, D. Valencia, B. Frazier and S. Paabo (1993)

"Genetic and linguistic differentiation in the Americas", Proceedings of the National Academy of Sciences, USA 90:10663-10667; A. Torroni and others (1993) "Asian Affinities and Continental Radiation of the four founding native American mt DNAs". *American Journal of Human Genetics* 53:563-90; and R.L. Cann (1994) mt DNA and native Americans. A Southern Perspective, *American Journal of Human Genetics* 55:7-11.

16. P. Menozzi, A. Piazza and L.L. Cavalli-Sforza (1978) "Synthetic maps of Human gene frequencies in Europeans", *Science* 201:786-79.
17. R.R. Sokal, N.L. Oden and C. Wilson (1991) "Genetic Evidence for the Spread of Agriculture in Europe by Demic Diffusion", *Nature* 351: 143-145; L.L. Cavalli-Sforza, A. Piazza and P. Menozzi (1994). "The History and Geography of Human Genes" Princeton, Princeton University Press.
18. A simulation study has in effect demonstrated that the only plausible alternative to the spread of farmers from the Near East followed by a limited intermixing with the populations encountered is the substitution of these populations by the farmers in the course of their expansion. A process of this kind does not have to have happened rapidly, nor in a violent form. What is important is that one can comprehend genetic variability in present populations also by postulating that these populations were formed from few individuals of Anatolian origin, without any contribution from those who were in Europe before the Neolithic period. Of course the fact that this model is compatible with the data does not imply that things happened in exactly this way. See G. Barbujani, R.R. Sokal and N.L. Oden (1995) Indo-European Origins; A Computer Simulation Test of Five Models, *American Journal of Physical Anthropology* 96:109-132.
19. Besides the quoted volume of 1987, by Colin Renfrew it is worth reading, "Before Babel: Speculations on the Origins of Linguistic Diversity", Cambridge *Archaeological Journal* I:3-23, Archaeology, Genetics and Linguistic Diversity, *Man* 27:445-78, and *World Languages and Human Dispersals. A minimalist view, in Transition to Modernity*, edited by J.A. Hall and I.C. Jarvie, pp. 11-68, Cambridge, Cambridge University Press.
20. G. Barbujani and A. Pilastro (1993) "Genetic Evidence on Origin and Dispersal of Human Populations Speaking Languages of the Nostratic Macrofamily", Proceedings of the National Academy of Sciences, USA 90:4670-4673; and G.B. Barbujani, A. Pilastro, S. DeDomenico and C. Renfrew (1994) "Genetic Variation in North

Africa and Eurasia. Neolithic and Demic Diffusion vs. Palaeolithic Colonisation", *American Journal of Physical Anthropology* 95:137-154.

21. S. Paabo (1995) "Molecular Cloning of Ancient Egyptian Mummy DNA", Nature 314:644-645:S Paabo, R.G. Higuchi and A.C. Wilson (1989) "Ancient DNA and the Polymerase Chain Reaction: The Emerging Field of Molecular Archaeology" *Journal of Biological Chemistry* 264:9709-9712.

3

Beyond Myths and Customs: Origins and Evolution of *Homo Sapiens*

Giorgio Manzi

The idea of modernity is commonly used nowadays. We associate it with "actuality", "progress" and "emancipation". In history, the term Modern Age includes a period of three centuries spanning the Renaissance to the French Revolution: after this period we find ourselves in the Recent or Contemporary ages. "Modernism" refers to those religious literary and artistic movements which accompanied the turn from the nineteenth to the twentieth century. "Modernism" also represents that tendency of detachment from tradition, for the adoption of new tastes and ideas—in the more or less implicit belief that new is better than old.

Usually, modern is opposed to ancient. We know then that this term does not define by itself the boundaries within which its meaning extends, as these can change according to which elements we chose to include in our 'before and after play'.

Recently, the necessity for the use of this term has also been felt by paleoanthropologists—in the expression "anatomically modern *Homo sapiens*" (a.m. *H. sapiens*) — extending its meaning enormously at least in chronological terms. From the "modernity" of the bourgeois revolution in the second millennium AD, time unravels, leading us to the "modernity" of another revolution or rather of an evolutionary transition in the history of our own species—the last major transition during the course of human evolution, one which has marked the passage from the archaic to those we call modern humans.

Towards the end of the Middle Pleistocene period, archaic humans—living in three continents (Asia, Africa and Europe) and both hemispheres, after a long evolutionary history—were subjected to selective pressures which influenced their biology and culture. In conditions of geographical isolation, populations diversified in regional morphotypes which had different histories and destinies. It is from this geographical dispersion and biological variability that emerged the human species we call a.m. *H. sapiens*; the new!

At this point, two questions arise. The first regards the use of the term modern as applied to the Linnaean classification. Isn't *H. sapiens* sufficient? Or, why don't we use the subspecies denomination *H. sapiens* as can be encountered in many texts and popular books? But in this last case, which are the other subspecies included in the species *H. sapiens* and why? For example, is *H. sapiens neanderhalensis* really a member of our species? From which species (or subspecies) do we and the Neanderthals derive? As we can see, from an apparently native question many others follow. It is always so in paleoanthropology.

The second question—the use of the term "anatomically" added to modern—could seem less important. What is the significance of this precision? What is anatomy? Are we perhaps alluding to its meaning as a partial component, macroscopic and exterior, of the phenotype? Are we dealing with humans which are anatomically but not genetically modern? Alternatively, do we just want to specify that they are modern but not recent humans anatomically similar to us even if not quite us? On the other hand, do we only want to leave cultural and behaviour aspects out from our arguments? Were the human beings only for what they appeared, and not for what they did?

In any case, the basic truth is that paleoanthropologists have acquired a more prudent attitude in naming new species in contrast to the time when the attribution of a binomial Latin name to each fossil specimen was in use. The examples could be infinite: *Pithecanthropus erectus*, *Sinanthropus pekinensis*, *Plesianthropus transvalensis*, *Telanthropus capensis*, *Zinjanthropus boised*. At the same time, paleoanthropologists are more familiar today with concepts, models and methods of the evolutionary biology. Following an interdisciplinary approach, the reconstruction of our natural history seems now possible, even from the scanty evidence which is available. This is therefore an important moment for paleoanthropology, in which once common stereotypes —like 'the fossil hunter' or 'the measurer of skulls'—seem now left behind.

In this study we will attempt to address some of the above issues while discussing the evidence concerning the last transition in the evolution of our species. In so doing, we will try to avoid falling into the "narrative trap" that Misia Landau[1] described some years ago. Through a dissection of the less technical components of the paleoanthropological literature and using the same critical tools Vladimir Prop used in the *Morphology of the Folktale.*[2] Landau's rigorous and systematic inquiry illuminated the fundamental structure, the narrative logic and the recurrent features frequently used by paleoanthropologists and unmasked the mythological identity which lies behind many descriptions and interpretations of fossils, datings and prehistory scenarios. For if nothing else, paleoanthropology answers to none other than the need of humanity to tell a fantastic story—and the most consolatory possible—of its own origins. But in virtue of the conceptual and methodological progress to which it has been alluded above, it is possible today to overcome this "juvenile" phase of our discipline and reach the more mature status of historical science.

Origins of the Genus *Homo*

At present[3] the appearance in the fossil record of the most ancient hominids can be dated to more than 4 million years ago, at a time not far from our evolutionary roots (about 6 million years ago) as is known from the comparative biomolecular analysis between extant human and African apes which can be compared from the contribution by G. Destro-Bisol in this same volume. In Western and Southern Africa, hominids of the genus *Australopithecus* evolved from semiarboreal apes adapting and diversifying in the African Savannahs. Bipedal locomotion is certainly the most interesting adaptation acquired in colonizing the new environment fundamental also for the next evolutionary step. Only late the gradual expansion of the brain accompanied the technological progress during the Palaeolithic as well as the development of the intellectual, behavioural and cultural capacities which are ours today.

Million of years after the main hominid adaptive radiation, with the appearance of the genus *Homo*, the diversity at interspecific level among hominids disappeared leaving place for geographical dispersion of a single species. During the last million years, archaic humans—morphologically and behaviourally referable to *Homo erectus* (*H. erectus*)—reached Western Asia and, moving to northern latitudes, also a greater part of Europe.

At the moment the most ancient remains commonly referred to *H. erectus* (cf. *Hommo ergaster*[4]) come from the sites near Lake Turkana in Kenya: the cranial remains called KNM-ET 3733 and 3883 and the famous Sariokotome juvenile skeleton (KNM-WT 15000) which is dated to 1.6 million years ago. By contrast, recent datings have attributed similar ages to some of the specimens found in Java[5] and China[6]. This evidence could be considered in contrast with the African origins of *H. erectus* or alternatively, may indicate a more remote (about 2 million years ago) hominid departure from Africa. Further in Europe, the human, presence at the beginning of the Pleistocene (2-1.5 million years ago) period, is claimed at both the Dmanist Georgian site[7] and that of Venta Micena near Orce in Spain.[8]

In all these cases, however, the most part of the specialists are not favourable at the moment in conferring decisive importance to such a still controversial evidence. For the time being, in the absence of convincingly disproving data we can consider Africa the place of appearance of the genus *Homo*. In Africa then the earliest populations of the most archaic forms of *Homo* (*H. rundolfensis*, *H. habilis*, *H. ergaster*) have been subjected to a selective pressure which favoured individuals with a bulky constitution, robust skeletal elements high endocranial volumes and possession of new lithe technologies. Successively, these hominids undertook an unprecedented geographic diffusion with the occupation through extremely diverse environments, through the adaptation to a wide range of ecological niches.

The archaeological record concerning *H. erectus* indicates the existence of a complex relationship among social organization, acquisition of new technologies and "cultural" transmission, such as, elaborate lithic instruments, indicating an increasing attention to symmetry and shape: hunting and butchering places: home bases showing a certain functional division of the living space: expressions of a relatively complex social life, etc. However, when observing this stage of human evolution the overall impression is one of a certain behavioural fixation. Many hundred thousands of years passed without major modifications, except for small variations from the original model presented by *H. erectus*: the archaeological record shows scarce variation in space and time, in contrast with the wide geographical distribution reached and (on a biological level) with the tendency towards increasing brain volumes.

Features Discernible in *H. erectus*

The posteranial and, especially, the cranial morphology which accompanied humans for over one million years, until the acquisition of modern anatomy, can be already recognized in the first appearances of *H. erectus* in Africa. During the last two decades specialists,[9] have been debating whether *H. erectus* can be considered a stable species in time, or if the rise in encephalic volume and other changes in the skeletal morphology should be taken in account to demonstrate a gradual pattern of evolution.

H. erectus' cranium is massive, with thick walls and low vault (platycephaly) characterized by a maximum width near the auditory channel, a robust supraorbital protuberance, a receding forehead and a marked postorbital constriction of the cranium (as seen from above), a steep profile of the parietal (from behind) and by a wedge shaped occipital (in lateral view), stretching itself posteriorly. The face is massive and large, with a pronounced prognatism both of the nasal and alveolar regions; the mandible presents a chin. *H. erectus* had large teeth, even if less than his ancestors; the incisors often assume a particular shovel shape (with a characteristic thickening of the inner sides of the teeth).

Equally, the postcranial skeleton is robust, with the lower limbs shorter than the thorax. Each part of the skeleton is particularly strong and the long bones' (such as the femur) medullar channel is reduced, due to the great development of the cortical structure. Size and weight are similar to modern human standards: for example, the teenager's Nariokotonie skeleton (KNMT 15000; about 1.6 million years old) is particularly tall for the age at death of this specimen, probably capable of reaching and exceeding 180 cm in height as an adult. Cranial capacity is high, with an average 1050 ml, which reaches the lower limit of present human variation.

The Evolution of *H. erectus*

H. erectus' destiny is controversial, and interlaced with several other stories — the evolution of the Neanderthals (in Europe and south-western Asia [the Levant]) for one side, and the origin of modern humans (probably in Africa), from another.

During the Middle-Pleistocene (between approximately 700 and 150 thousand years ago [Kyr BPl], heterogeneous human morphotypes of uncertain phylogenetic and taxonomic collocation emerged throughout the Old World. They represent transitional morphologies between *H. erectus* and *H. sapiens*, referable in several ways both to the archaic and modern species. In conformity with a nomenclature still common in popular books and text books — which implies a gradualist interpretation of the evolution of the genus *Homa*[10]—the fossils of this period are attributed to the so-called "archaic *H. sapiens*". The evolution and the diversification of this archaic humanity, belonging to and/or descending from *H. erectus*, can be followed both in Africa and in Eurasia for several hundred thousands of years.

The morphological diversity among the Mid-Pleistocene human fossil samples doesn't allow for a univocal description and makes their attribution to a unique taxon inappropriate, except if in a provisional and conventional manner (as for the doubtful "archaic *H. sapiens*"); since many specimens have uncertain datings, the picture appears further complicated. Still hominids between *H. erectus* and *H. sapiens* show an important common characteristic: the phenomenon known as "encephalisation" consisting in the enlargement of the cranial vault and the increasing brain size. At the end of this evolutionary trend (that is after the end of the Middle Pleistocene) we find specimens like Kabwe, Ndutu e Jebel

Irhoud (Africa), or Ngandong Dali e Jinniushan (Asia) which differ in the mixture of archaic and derived traits, but share greater endocranial volumes than their ancestors. Cranial capacity of these humans reaches and exceeds 1300 ml on an average; fully within current human range of variation.

A Particular Case Study of Human Evolution in Europe

Thanks to over a century of research and discoveries—the result of a particular attention to prehistory, which could be defined "curocentric"—human evolution in Europe during the last million years is perhaps the best known case now. During the first half of this century, theories were formulated about a hypothetical parallel evolution between Neanderthal and modern humans in Europe during the Middle Pleistocence. Authors like Sir Arthur Keith, Henri Vallois, Sergio Sergi, supposed in fact the coexistence in Europe of two different lineages: the Neanderthal on one side, and the *pre sapiens* (or the Probhaneranthropi, as Sergi[12] called them) on the other. The latter group would have given rise to modern *H. sapiens* during last quaternary glaciation, and are represented by the upper Palaeolithic specimens such as those from Cro-Magnon, Combe Capelle, Chancelade, Oberkassel, Predmost, etc. The Neanderthals took the role of "degenerative variants" in human evolution, an interpretation which lasted until the 50s when a sort of rehabilitation was reached, which conferred the Neanderthals the status of *H. sapiens neanderthalensis*.

More recently, in contrast, human evolution in Europe has been interpreted as an example of regional anagenetic sequence, showing a gradual and directional pattern of evolution. European populations belonging to *H. erectus* or *H. heidelbergensis* according to some authors,[13] isolated for prolonged periods in this geographical *cul-de-sao* gradually assumed peculiar anatomic characteristics and adaptations fully expressed during the last quaternary glaciation by the so-called "classic" or Wurmian Neanderthals. The extreme morphological homogeneity observed in these late European archaic humans seemingly implies rigid selective pressures and reproductive isolation. Few specialists still believe in a "Neanderthal phase" of human evolution. The origins of a.m. *H. sapiens* must be sought elsewhere.

Hominid presence in Europe could have begun well before half million years ago, even if a relevant fossil documentation has long been missing. However, between August and September 1995 fossil evidence has been described from Lower/Middle Pleistocene sites in Spain and Italy: samples of extraordinary interests which must still be subjected to an exact morphological identification and dating. They both could date back to 700 kyr BP. In Spain, fragmentary remains are referable to several individuals from the site of Gran Dolina[14] in Atapuerca, near Burgos. The finding in Italy (at Ceprano, Frosinone in 1994) concern a siagle incomplete cranium,[15] the morphology resulting after a long and patient work of restoration, is quite surprising in our continental context—a European *H. erectus* has been for the first time discovered? In any case, archaeological evidence of human presence in Europe before 500 kyr BP has never lacked, and could be older than the new fossils we just mentioned: the Italian site of Isernia-La Pineta is an example of that. There are also French and Spanish sites, with archaic lithic assemblages, dating more than one million years.

Until recently, the most ancient human fossils obtained was the mandible from Mauer, found near Heidelberg in Germany in 1907, referable to 650-450 kyr BP. Even if only for the morphology of the mandible and the teeth of the lower arch, the Mauer mandible shows characteristics of the African and Asiatic forms of *H. erectus*. The Boxgrove tibia from the English Channel's coast has probably the same ago.

We must wait hundred thousand years for the European fossil record to increase considerably: the fragmentary cranial remains, about 400 kyr BP, in Bilzinsgleben (East Germany); the Vertesszollos' occipital bone (near Budapest); the series of remains from Caume de l' Arago (French Pyrences); the teeth from Fontana Ranuccio (Italy). The massive cranium of Petralona (accidentally found in 1960 in a cave of the Calcydic Peninsula, Greece) could be of the same ago. The human sample of this period starts to show regional evolutionary trends forwards the Neanderthal features. Some archaic characteristics weaken (*plesiomorphies*, technically speaking), while some derived (*apomorphic*) Neanderthal traits begin to appear.

This process is more evident in the European fossils of the successive age from about 350 kyr BP to the last quaternary glaciation: the Wiirm (which began almost 80 kyr BP). Atapuerca (Spain), Forbe's Quarry (Gibraltar), Biache, Fontecchevade and La Chaise (France), Swanscombe (Great Britain), Steinheim and Ehringdorf (Germany), Castel di Guido and Saccopastore (Italy), Krapina (ex Yugoslavia) are some of the key-sites for our knowledge of this phase of human evolution in Europe. Mainly to these remains we owe the conclusion that in Europe, exclusively, we assist to the progressive appearance of the Neanderthal features, during the long chronological gap preceding the Wurmian glaciation. The appearance of these features, however, is not homogeneous—this is in fact called "mosaic" evolution, implying that each trait could or not be combined with others on the same fossil, or could be differently present in contemporary remains and produce heterogeneous morphologies even in a same site at the same time.

This conclusion has obtained a considerable confirmation from the Sima de los Huesos (literally "bone quarry") near Atapuerca in northern Spain,[16] the fossil sample discovered there, belonging to almost 24 individuals, is dated to about 300 kyr BP. It is the most complete and informative evidence for the "mosaic" appearance of Neanderthal morphologies during a stage which once was simply not possible to take in adequate consideration. Could it coincide with the dating of Altamura? The human skeleton with archaic morphology accidentally found in October 1993 near Altamura in the Murgia of Bari,[17] represents another recent discovery: extraordinary for its antiquity, completeness and characteristics. If the Altamura skeleton should show the same antiquity of those of the Atapuerca's site (300 kyr BP instead 400 or 200) we should have the opportunity of a comparison between untidy remains of several individuals (in Spain) and a single individual, comprising all its skeletal components (in Italy).

An Overviewing of the Neanderthals

Exclusively distributed in Europe and in the Levant, the Neanderthals were skilful hunters, of a medium-low stature and a massive build. Except for the anatomically modern samples of the

Upper Palaeolithic, Neanderthals are certainly the best known fossil hominids at least enough to provide us with indications on demography and life cycle parameters.[18]

Concerning the physical aspect, the Neanderthal cranium has an archaic structure, but its size (especially the endocranial volume: over 1500 ml on average) is similar to that of modern humans: however, the vault is long and wide but not high. Seen from behind, the skull presents a typical rounded profile (called *en bombe*); the receding forehead follows the double but continuous supraobitary arches: the occipital has a typical eminence called *chignon* (or "bunning"). The face is characterized by a particular mid-facial prognatism, an unmistakable morphology in which the maxillary region is expanded, the check-bones slant backwards and the dental arches protrude anteriorly. The orbits are large and rounded, the nasal cavity is large and the chin is absent. The front teeth show strong wear (for extra-alimentary use) and molars and premolars are "taurodont" (with enlargement of the pulp cavity). The Neanderthals showed also peculiar characteristics of the trunk and the limbs. The shoulder articulation, for example, include a typical conformation of the scapula favouring the abduction and flexion of the arms. The bones of the hands seem well adapted for a particularly effective grasp in relationship with both technologies for tool production and hunting activities. Another aspect regards the particular conformation of the pelvis, which in females appears "larger" than that of recent women.

The overall morphological pattern of the European Wurmian Neanderthals is also represented in the Near Eastern Neanderthals, found in sites between Palestine and Caucasian area; but in this case some Neanderthal features are less pronounced. The same incomplete morphological expression is observed in older European specimens, such as the interglacial fossils from Saccopastore, found in Rome on the banks of the Aniene river nearly 50 years ago. This has led to the hypothesis[19] that the Neanderthal variability in the Levant had a European origin "at the time of Saccopastore" (almost 120 kyr BP) and evolved independently from the typical Neanderthals of continental and Mediterranean Europe.

If the evolution of the Neanderthals in Europe seems now

sufficiently described, many questions concerning their destiny remain still open. As a consequence, the question whether Neanderthals should be considered a member of our own species (as *H. sapiens neanderthalensis*) —if not an independent new species (*H. neanderthalensis*)—has been recently opened again. This question is closely related to our main goal: the question of modern human origins and the relationship of the new species (or sub-species?) with the last archaic hominids (Neanderthals included).

The Origin/s of Modern *H. sapiens*

During the last decade, the reconstruction of the events which brought the appearance of the extant human species (*H. sapiens*) has been at the centre of a renewed intense discussion within the scientific community of paleoanthropologists,[20] furthermore, the theoretical and interpretative aspects which the problem of our origins as a species involves have been topics of interest for evolutionary biologists in general. Although it is the fossil evidence itself to inspire the pertinent hypotheses the anthropological record concerning the first appearance of anatomically modern humans (or a.m. *H. sapiens*) is also compared and integrated with current ideas and pardigms, archaeological and paleoecological data, information derived from the genetic diversity of living populations.

There are two main opposing views. The first one—which comes from the traditional interpretation of the evolution of the genus *Homo*, known as *candelabrum model*—is the multiregional evolution theory.[21] The second one on the other hand does not support an ancient origin of present human diversity and is conversely inspired by the hypothesis of a recent African origin,[22] that is a localized and rapid emergence in Africa followed by a worldwide geographical diffusion. These two opposing working hypotheses can be referred as "multiregional" and "diffusionist" respectively.

Specifically, the multiregional model asserts that anatomically modern populations evolved in Africa, Asia and Europe with substantial continuity with the preceding archaic populations (*H. erectus*?, *H. heidelbergensis*?, *arachaic H. sapiens*?) in their respective geographical areas. This hypothesis is based on a gradualist vision of evolution: present human diversity is seen as the result of small and constant changes within each continental population, which in turn was derived from the geographic diffusion of *H. erectus*. The occurrence of intense gene flow would have allowed the different populations and geographic variants to maintain the species "unity" preventing extreme forms of differentiation and contributing to the spread of favourable mutations.[23]

On the other hand, the diffusionist model assumes that the transition from *H. erectus* (and/or derived forms) to a.m. *H. sapiens* took place in a restricted area, somewhere between south-eastern Africa and the Levant. It assumes also that the transition came about in relatively recent times, something like 200 kyr BP. Thereafter, during its successive geographical expansion the modern species diffused to all the continents, replacing the pre-existent archaic populations without significantly mingling with them. The replacement of the archaic populations by the modern ones could be explained in several ways and in any case, in terms of adaptive competition. This proposal is in agreement with a discontinuous course of the evolutionary process characterized by long periods of "stasis", alternated with rapid and crucial speciation events: therefore it is consistent with the evolutionary theory known as "punctuated equilibria" introduced by Stephen J. Gould and Niles Eldredge in the seventies.[24]

From a genetic standpoint, the multiregional model necessarily assumes that continent by continent, there has been a substantial morphological, and therefore genetic continuity between prehistoric and modern populations, and that present human diversity has its origin in the geographical dispersion of *H. erectus* from well over one million years ago. On the other hand, the diffusionist model leads to the consideration of current genetic variability as the result of a rather recent process begun not long before 200 kyr BP, interpreting the evidence for morphological continuity between archaic and modern populations outside Africa, as a common, but independent persistence of ancestral features (*symplesiomorphies*).

There are also other working hypotheses which hold somewhat intermediate positions besides these two extreme models. For example, it is suggested that modern humans actually appeared in

Africa at the time proposed by the diffusionist model, but that during the subsequent geographical diffusion, the modern gene-pool significantly mingled with that of the archaic populations at least somewhere. It could have occurred principally assimilating them according to a hypothesis called "hybridization and replacement" or being assimilated according to the "assimilation" model.[26] In short, the various models distinguish themselves for the relative importance each attributes to the contrasting phenomena of archaic/modern population replacement versus genetic continuity between fossil and recent humans in the various regions.

If we try to define the framework offered by the fossil record at our disposal—in order to assess the consistency of the various models on modern human origin/s—we obtain a rather articulated, sometimes contradictory picture in which the same evidence may lead to such diverse interpretations as to support one or another alternative model.

Fossil samples which could prove a transition from archaic humans to a.m. *H. sapiens* earlier than elsewhere have been found in Africa. These are fossils of essentially modern anatomy—found at the sites of Omo Kibish (in Ethiopia), Border Cave and Klasies River Mouth (in South Africa)—which could be referred to an age between 130 and 80 kyr BP. However, element of the greatest controversy is not their anatomy, rather the reliability of their dating which if confirmed would make them the most ancient evidence for modern humans.

The dating obtained towards the end of eighties for the Palestinian sites of Oafzeh and Skhul, in Israel (about 100 kyr BP),[27] are instead considered reliable. It can then be deduced that the first modern humans from the Levant were both chronological consistent with an African origin of a.m. *H sapiens* and 20 to 40 thousand years older than many Neanderthal specimens from the same region. These unexpected dates have literally subverted the criteria by which the Neanderthals had been considered ancestral to modern humans, at least in that region. A more acceptable hypothesis is that these two different humanities experienced a long period of contact and interaction (presumably competitive in ecological terms) before the complete transition to fully modern populations.

The currently available picture for Eastern Asia and Australia seems to indicate, more than anywhere else, the presence of transitional forms between *H. erectus* and some other type of archaic humans by some referred to as archaic *H. sapiens*".[28] On the other hand, the elements of continuity between these archaic humans and a.m. *H. sapiens*, based on the regional persistence of some minor anatomical features are instead more controversial. According to some researchers,[29] in Central Europe as well, the fossil evidence suggests a certain degree of continuity between the Neanderthal and the first anatomically modern populations. However, in other areas of the European continent, the transition appears more sudden and does not match with hypotheses of an evolution *in situ* or more generally speaking, of regional biological continuity.

In any case, one should also focus on a higher level of morphological variation, such as for instance the overall shape, i.e., the architecture and the basic structure of the skull. Thus, in all geographical regions we observe a relatively sudden change, from a typically low and elongated cranial vault to that of modern humans, characterized by a vertical elevation of the forehead, of the parietals and of the occipital region. This kind of rapid and structural morphological change appears to be difficult to interpret in terms of "multiregional evolution" (one must recur to somewhat finalistic views, or claim evolutionary parallelisms): rather, it favours the hypothesis of diffusion from a single centre of origin.[30]

Aside from the fossil record during the course of the past decade, important archaeological and paleoecological evidence (datings included) has become available for a more accurate definition of this problem. Moreover, researches concerning the genetic[31] and linguistic[32] variability of extant populations have had an increasing impact on our knowledge on past evolutionary events. In light of this information, and according to the so-called "molecular clock"[33] it appears possible to reconstruct and interpret the principal stages in the evolution of our species, such as size of the founder population, time of its differentiation, successive events of population growth, geographical diffusion and further differentiation (refer to the contributions by G. Destro-Bisol and G. Barbujani in this same volume). The kind of evidence appeared in the last decade from this side[34] seems to favour the hypotheses based on a recent African origin assumption and contradicts those behind the multiregional theory. As has already seen, the fossils and other paleontological evidence are not in contrast with this interpretation rather they seem to support it. Thus, an increasing number of researchers agree at present about the principal stages of *H. sapiens'* successive diffusion in some way similar to that migration routes followed by *H. erectus* one million years earlier. In short, modern humans would have originated in sub-Saharan Africa around 200 kyr BP, then expanded and diffused in the African continent, then to the Levant at about 100 kyr BP, to the Far East and Australia before 50 kyr BP, and finally to Europe after 50 kyr BP.

If all of this will be confirmed (or "not disproved"), we should have a convincing picture of modern human origins, inclined towards the diffusionist model. That is, a scenario based on a rather defined event, both in place and time, followed by geographical diffusion and replacement, more or less complete, of the archaic populations of Africa, Mediterranean Asia, Far East and Europe. In this scenario, the destiny of the archaic *taxa* of the genus *Homo* is that of partial or complete extinction leaving place for the modern one. A picture of competition for survival takes shape, possibly partially relieved by some degree of interbreeding between populations. From this same picture, we also infer an adaptive (and reproductive) advantage in a.m. *H. sapiens*, possibly by virtue of our species, cultural capabilities. Taking a closer look at Europe and the Levani, there are grounds to predict that the degree of hybridization between archaic and modern populations was small if any. By this reasoning it is difficult to still support the idea of the Neanderthals and *H. sapiens* belonging to the same species. In this perspective, *H. sapiens* have been considered so far as a combination of too heterogeneous prehistoric human forms grouped in a single *taxon*. These should instead be distinguished as different species both between themselves and from the modern one. Perhaps, the Neanderthals can be returned (with their direct ancestors) to *H. neanderthalensis*.

There is however more. The origin and diffusion of modern humans are, according to some authors[35] a too complex and articulated issue to be satisfactorily explained by either the extremely gradualist approach behind the multiregional model or the rigidly diffusionist positions. The mutual exclusion between the two models — though useful in a first stage of discussion — appears outdated; both hypotheses try to oversimplify the issue presenting it as a single, indivisible problem, devoid of the complexity of the evolutionary processes concerning a particular, i.e., cultural species amongst mammals; our own. These processes — which involved populations of three continents for probably more than hundred thousand years — could have followed different pathways according to the different geographical areas and chronologies. In this light, the global problem of the origins of *H. sapiens* could be subdivided into a succession of secondary stages which could be tested or "confuted" separately. Generally speaking, one can expect that in different regions, the degree of replacement of the archaic gene-pool with that of the modern one—and, vice versa, the degree of regional continuity—has been proportional, firstly, to the geographical distance of that particular region from the centre of origin of the modern species, and secondly, to the time span passed from the origin of the new phenotype to the archaic/modern contact.[36]

An element which raises further complexity arises from the archaeological record. Far from illustrating a reassuring bio-cultural parallelism in which the appearance of the modern anatomy corresponds, for example, to a substantial change in the production of lithic,[37] the elements now available include a simple interpretation. However, even if the interpretative models used until recently seem outdated for a sufficiently sophisticated description of the phenomenon of the transition,[38] it is not necessarily expected that a biological novelty should immediately manifest its "cultural" behavioural, technological social, etc.,— potentials. The contrast between archaic and modern humans during their subsequent contacts have had archaeological interpretations such as, for example, a plausible Neanderthal acculturation[39] have been real in the evidence coming from various sites throughout Europe.[40]

In any case, however, the evolution of the modern species may have taken place, we know that from 25-30 kyr BP, archaic populations are no longer represented in the fossil record, although a significant part of their genes may possibly persist in several regions. In Europe, for example, after the disappearance of the Neanderthals from the fossil record, we find individuals whose skeleton has acquired all the observable characteristics of recent populations (S. Sergi used for them the expression Phaneranthropi). On a comparative level, it can be useful to highlight that the modern cranium presents, since the earliest stages, a greater vertical elevation then ever, with capacities varying around 1450 ml. Consequences of the elevation of the cranial vault are a steeper forehead, parallel sides of the cranium and a rounded occipital region, particularly accentuated bone superstructures disappear as the brow ridges, for example, loose in robusticity. The facial size reduces and the profile is shorter, moreover, several elements of gracility appear in the structures of the face and jaw, now presenting a chin.

Dealing with modern humans, we face now a remarkable phenotypic diversity arisen during the course of time, which often poses us with morphological exceptions, however minor, to the general rule. Moreover, it is known that after the appearance of the first anatomically modern populations, the species has undergone an increasing gracilization of the skeleton. Bones and teeth from extant populations are less robust than those of archaic humans, such as the Neanderthals, but, also of the first Palaeolithic representatives of the modern species. This is likely due to the effects of a decrease in dependence on physical strength for survival but it is also probable that other factors have contributed to decreasing robusticity such as the increase in population density, starting from the Neolithic, and the related incidence of weakening factors like famines, epidemics, etc.[41]

During the upper Palaeolithic an unprecedented cultural explosion is observed, in which, apart from a massive and innovative production of lithies, first symbolic expressions are encountered. With respect to the middle Palaeolithic, the hypologies and techniques in production of lithics multiply and differentiate rapidly and the archaeological record is enriched by tools presenting elongated shapes, produced with an unknown capacity for variation. The first artistic manifestations also appear in rock paintings and engravings, carved ornamental domestic articles, pendants and other objects for personal ornamentation. Within this rapid cultural progress the beginning of an exponential evolution is distinguished which will lead within few tens of thousands years, from the Palaeolithic to the Neolithic, to the Iron Age and to the History.

REFERENCES

1. Landau, M., 1984, Human Evolution as Narrative, *American Scientist*, 72: 265.
2. Propp, V., 1928, Morfologija Skazki, Acadiemia, Leningrado.
3. White, T.D., Suwa, G. and Asfaw, B., 1991, *Australopithecus ramidus*, a new species of early hominid from Aramis, Ethiopia. *Nature*, 371: 306-312. Leakey, M.G., Feibel, C.S., Mc Dougall, I. & Walker, A. 1995—New four million-year-old-hominid species from Kanapoi and Allia Bay Kenya, *Nature* 376:565-71.
4. Swisher III C.C., Curtis G.H., Jacob, T., Getty, A.G., Supprijo A. and Widiasmoro, 1994, Age of the Earliest Known Hominids in Java, Indonesia, *Nature*, 263: 1118-21.
5. Wanpo, H., Ciochon, R., Yumin, G., Larick, R., Qiren, F., Schwarez, H., Yonge, C., de Vos J. and Rink, W., 1995, Early *Homo* and associated artefacts from Asia, *Nature*, 378: 221-320.
6. Gabunial and Vekua, A., 1995, A Plio-Pleistocene hominid from Dmanisi East Georgia Caucasus, *Nature*, 373: 509-512.
7. Gibert, J., Ribot, F., Ferrandez, C., Martinez, B., Caporicei, R. and Campillo, D., 1989, Anatomical study: Comparison of the Cranial Fragment from Venta Micena (Qree. Spain) with fossil and extant mammals, *Human Evolution*, 4: 283-305.
8. Wood, B., 1992, Origin and evolution of the genus *Homo, Nature*, 355: 783-790.
9. Eldredge, N. and Tattersall, I., 1982, The Myths of Human Evolution. Columbia University Press, New York, Cronin, J.E., Boaz, N.T., Stringer, C.B. and Rak, Y., 1981, Tempo and mode in hominid evolution, *Nature*, 292: 113-122.
10. Henneberg, M., and Thackeray, J.E., 1995, In *Evolutionary Theory*, 16(1).
11. Stringer, C.B., Hublin, J.J. and Vandermeersch, B., 1984, The origin of anatomically modern humans in Western Europe. In Smith F. and Spencer F. (eds.), *The Origins of Modern Humans: A World Survey of the Fossil Evidence*; pp. 51-135, A.R. Liss, New York.

12. Sergi, S., 1962, Morphological position of the "Prophaneranthropi" (Swanscombe and Fontechevade). In Howells W.W. (ed.), *Ideas on Human Evolution: Selected Essays 1949-1961*; pp. 507-520, Harvard University Press, Cambridge.
13. Stringer, C.B., 1994, Out of Africa: A Personal History. In M.H. Niteeki and D.V. Niteeki (eds), *Origins of Anatomically Modern Humans*: pp. 149-172. Plenum Press, New York.
14. Carbonell, E., Bermudez de Castro J.M., Arsuaga J.L., Diez J.C., Rosas A., Cuenca, Bescos G., Sala R. Mosquera M. & Rodriguez P., 1995, Lower Pleistocene hominids and artifacts from Atapuerca-TD6 (Spain), *Science*, 269: 826-830.
15. Ascenzi, A., Biddittu I., Cassoli, P.F., Segre A.G. and Segree Naldini E., 1985, Middle Pleistocene Human Calvaria, Central Italy, *Congreso Internacional de Paleontologia Humana*. Los Hominidos y su Entorno en el Pleistoceno Inferiory Medio Europeo (Orce. Sept., 1995). Circular: 83 (abstract).
16. Arsuaga, J.L. Martinez, I., Gracia, A., Carretero, J.M. & Carbonell E., 1993, Three new human skulls from the Sima de los Huesos Middle Pleistocene site in Sierra de Atapuerca. Spain, *Nature*, 362: 534-537.
17. Pesce-Delfino, V. and Vacca E., 1993, An Archaic Human Skeleton Discovered at Altamura (Bari, Italy), *Rivista di Antropologia*, 71: 249-257.
18. Trinkaus, E. and Tompkins, R.L., 1990, The Neanderthal Life Cycle: The Possibility, Probability and Perceptibility of Contrasts with Recent Humans. In C.J. DeRousseau (ed.). *Primate Life History and Evolution*; pp. 153-180. Wiley-Liss, New York.
19. Condemi, S., 1988, A review and analysis of the Riss-Wiirm Saccopastore skulls. Can they provide evidence in regard to the origin of Near Eastern Neanderthals? In F Trinkaus (ed.). L Homme de Neanderthal. vol. 3: L Anatomie; pp. 39-48. Etudes et Recherches Archeologiques de I' Universite de Liege n. 30. Liege.
20. Smith, F.H. and Spencer, F., (eds.), 1984, *The Origins of Modern Humans: A World Survey of the Fossil Evidence*, A.R. Liss, New York. Mellars, P.A. and Stringer, C.B. (eds.), 1989, *The Human Revolution Behavioural and Biological Perspective on the Origins of Modern Humans*. Edinburgh University Press, Edinburgh. Trinkaus, E. (ed.), 1989, The Emergence of Modern Humans. Biocultural Adaptations in the Later Pleistocence. Cambridge University Press, Cambridge. Brauer, G. and Smith, F.H. (eds.), *Continuity or Replacement. Controversies in Homo sapiens evolution*. A.A. Balkema Rotterdam, Hublin, J.J. & Tillier A.M. (eds.), 1992. Aux Origines de la Diversite

Humaine, Nouvelle Encyclopedie des Sciences et des Techniques. Presses Universitaires de France, Paris. Nitecki M.H. and Nitecki D.V. (eds.), 1994, *Origins of Anatomically Modern Humans*, Plenum Press, New York.

21. Wolpoff, M.H., Wu Xinzhi & Thorne, A.G., 1984, Modern *Homo sapiens* Origins: A General Theory of Hominid Evolution Involving the Fossil Evidence from East Asia. In Smith E.H. and Spencer F. (eds.), *The Origins of Modern Humans: A World Survey of the Fossil Evidence*; pp. 411-83. A.R. Liss, New York, Wolpoff M.H., 1989, Multiregional Evolution: The Fossil Alternative to Eden. In P.A. Mellars and C.B. Stringer (eds.), *The Human Revolution: Behavioural and Biological Perspective on the Origins of Modern Humans*, pp. 62-108, Edinburgh University Press, Edinburgh.
22. Stringer, C.B. and Andrews, P., 1988, Genetic and fossil evidence for the origin of modern humans, *Science*, 239: 1263-68.
23. Van Valen, L.M., 1986, Speciation and our own species, *Nature*, 322: 412.
24. Gould, S.J. & Eldredge, N., 1977, Punctuated equilibria: The Tempo and Mode of Evolution Reconsidered, *Paleobiology*, 3: 115-151.
25. Brauer, G., 1992, Africa's place in the evolution of *Homo sapiens*. In Brauer G. and Smith F.H. (eds.), *Continuity or Replacement. Controversies in Homo sapiens Evolution*, pp. 83-98. A.A. Balkema, Rotterdam.
26. Smith, F.H., Falsetti, A.B. and Donnelly, S.M., 1989, Modern Human Origins, *Yearbook of Physical Anthropology*, 32: 35-68.
27. Stringer, C.B., 1988, The Dates of Eden, *Nature*, 331: 565-66.
28. Pope, G.G., 1992, Craniofacial Evidence for the Origin of Modern Humans in China, *Yearbook of Physical Anthropology*, 35: 243-98.
29. Frayer, D.W., Wolpoff M.H., Thorne, A.G., Smith F.H. and Pope, G.G., 1993, Theories of Modern Human Origins: The Paleontological Test, *American Anthropologist*, 95: 15-50.
30. Manzi, G. Vienna, A. and Hauser, G., 1996, Developmental Stress and Cranial Hyposotosis Evaluated by Epigenetic Trait Occurrence and Distribution. An Exploratory Study on the Italian Neanderthals, *Journal of Human Evolution*, 30(6). Manzi G. 1996—Anagenesis and cladogenesis different patterns of evolution at the transition between archaic and modern humans. In *Los Hominidos y su entorno en el Pleistoceno inferior y medio Europeo* Proc. of the Congreso Internat de Paleont. Humana (Orce. Sept. 1995), in press.
31. Cann, R.L., Stoneking, M. and Wilson, A.C., 1987, Mitochondrial DNA and Human Evolution, *Nature*, 325: 31-36.
32. Cavalli Sforza, L.L., Piazza, A., Menozzi, P. and Mountain, I., 1988,

Reconstruction of Human Evolution: Bringing Together Genetic, Archaeological and Linguistic data, *Proceedings of the National Academy of Sciences, USA.*, 85: 6002-6006.

33. Harpending, H., 1994, Gene Frequencies, DNA Sequences, and Human Origins, *Perspectives in Biology and Medicine*, 37: 384-94.
34. Tattersall, I., 1986, Species Recognition in Human Paleontology, *Journal of Human Evolution*, 15: 165-175.
35. Aiello, L.C., 1993, The Fossil Evidence for Modern Human Origins in Africa: A Revised View, *American Anthropologist*, 95: 73-96.
36. Manzi, G., Grimaldi, S. and Destro-Bisol G., 1994, Modern Human Origin/s: Fossil, Genetic and Archaeological Evidence. State of the Art, *Rivista di Antropologia*, 72: 243-69.
37. Yellen, J.E., Brooks, A.S., Cornelissen, E., Mehlman, M.J. and Stewart, K., 1995, 'A Middle Stone Age Worked Bone Industry from Katanda, Upper Semliki Valley, Zaire', *Science*, 268: 553-56.
38. Bietti, A., 1991, 'Normal Science and Paradigmatic Biases in Italian Hunter-Gatherer Pre-history'. In G.A. Clark (ed.), *Perspectives on the Past: Theoretical Biases in Mediterranean Hunter-Gatherer Research*, 258-81. University of Pennsylvania Press, Philadelphia.
39. Mellars, P.A., 1989, 'Major issues in the emergence of modern humans', *Current Anthropology*, 30: 349-85.
40. Manzi, G. and Passarello, P., 1995, 'At the archaic modern boundary of the genus *Homo*: the Neanderthals from Grotta Breuil', *Current Anthropology*, 36: 355-66.
41. Macchiarelli, R. and Bondioli, L., 1986, 'Post Pleistocene Reduction in Human Dental Structure: A Reappraisal in Terms of Increasing Population Density', *Human Evolution*, I: 405-418.
42. Haeckel, E., 1891, *Anthropogenie*, W. Engelmann, Leipzig.
43. Ardrey, R., 1961, *African Genesis*, Collins, London.
44. Howells, W.W., 1959, *Mankind in the Making: The Story of Human Evolution*, Doubleday and C., New York.
45. Weidenreich, F., 1946, Apex. *Giants and Man*, University of Chicago Press, Chicago.
46. Stringer, C.B., 1992, Replacement Continuity and the Origin of *Homo sapiens*, In G. Brauer and F.H. Smith (eds.), *Continuity or Replacement: Controversies* in *Homo Sapiens Evolution*; pp. 9-24. A.A. Balkema, Rotterdam.
47. Howells, W.W., 1992, The dispersion of modern humans. In S. Jones R. Martin and D. Pilbeam (eds.), *The Cambridge Encyclopedia of Human Evolutions*; pp. 389-401. Cambridge University Press, Cambridge.

Fig. 1 : The humankind at the top of the evolutionary tree as it was represented at the end of nineteenth century.[42]

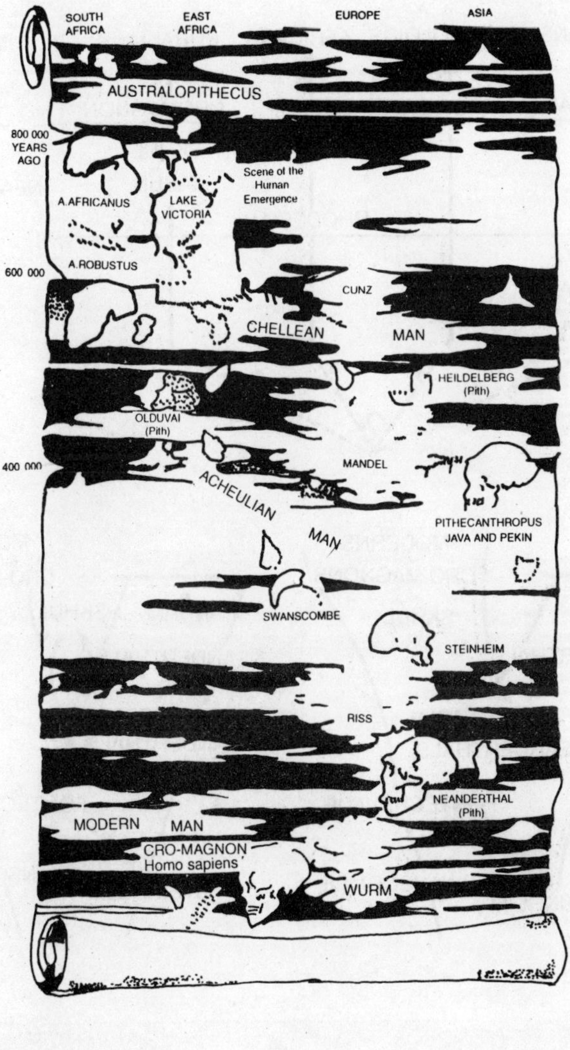

Fig. 2 : From the Serengenti's plains to the Slalom of Paleolithic hominids between the quaternary glaciations (Giinz. Mindel, Riss and Wiirm): A popular vision of human evolution according to our knowledge on this topic at the first half of this century.[43]

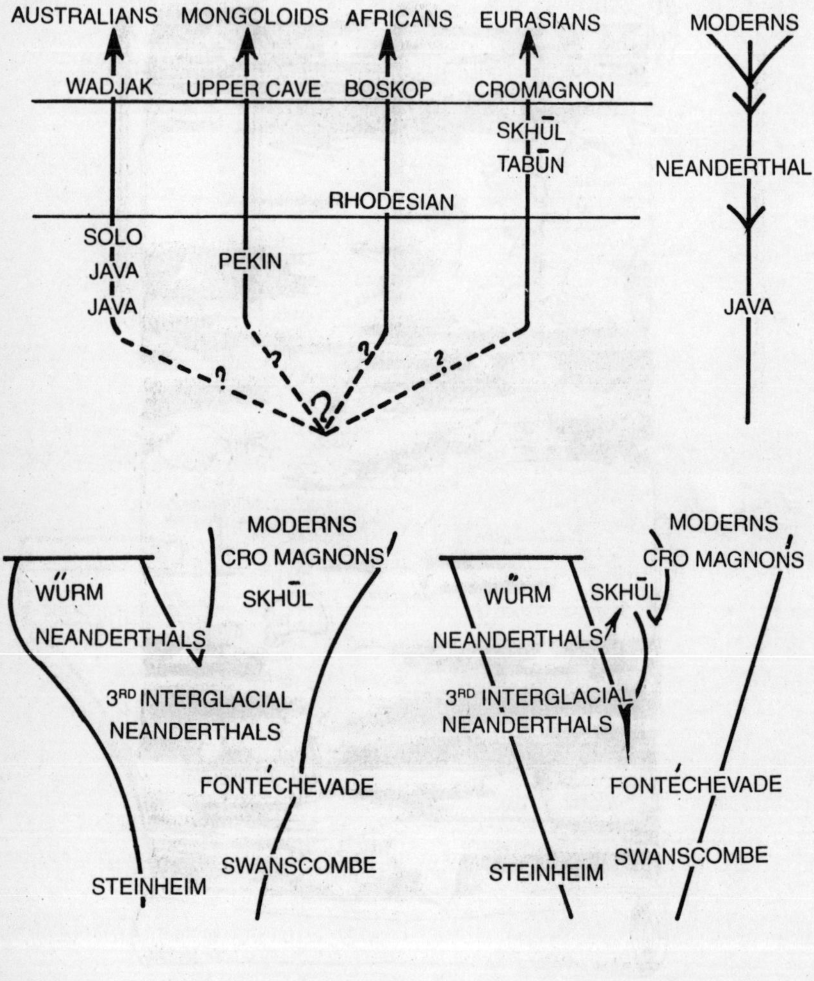

Fig. 3 : The classical W.W. Howells representation of different hypotheses on modern human origins at the end of the fifties.[44] From above (left): The so called "candelabrum model" by F. Weidenreich,[45] source of the current *multiregional* theory; an almost nineteenth-century hypothesis of linear sequence; two different varieties of the European 'pre-sapiens' theory.

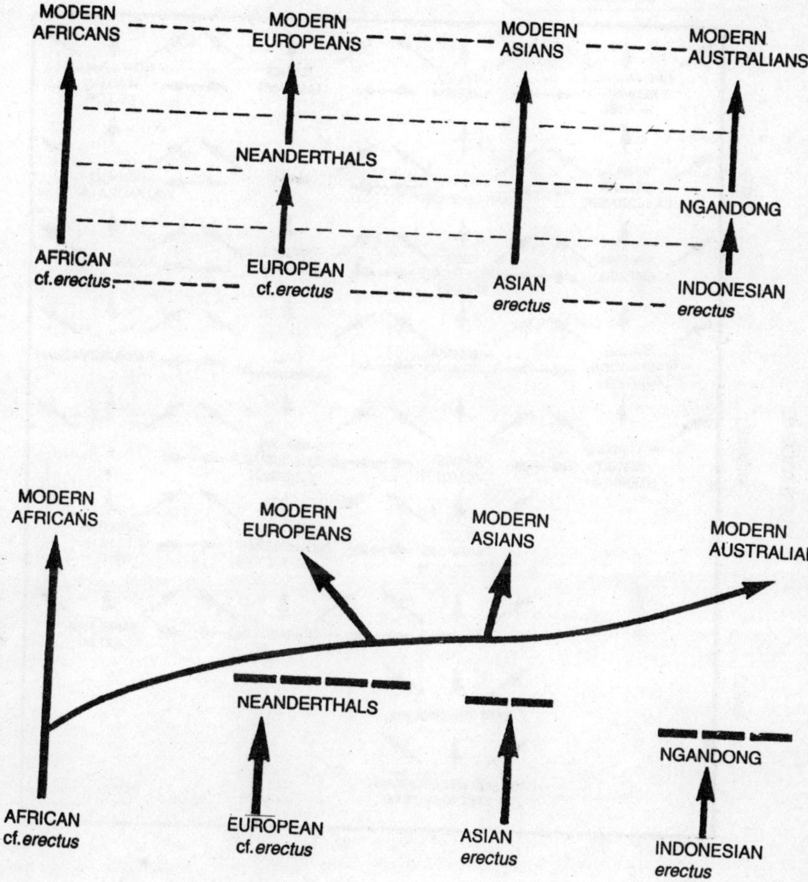

Fig. 4 : The two alternative hypotheses on the origin/s of modern humans as represented by C.B. Stringer.[46] Above: The regional continuity suggested by the *multiregional* model (the sketched lines show the gene flow between populations); below: The *diffusionist* model of a recent African origin.

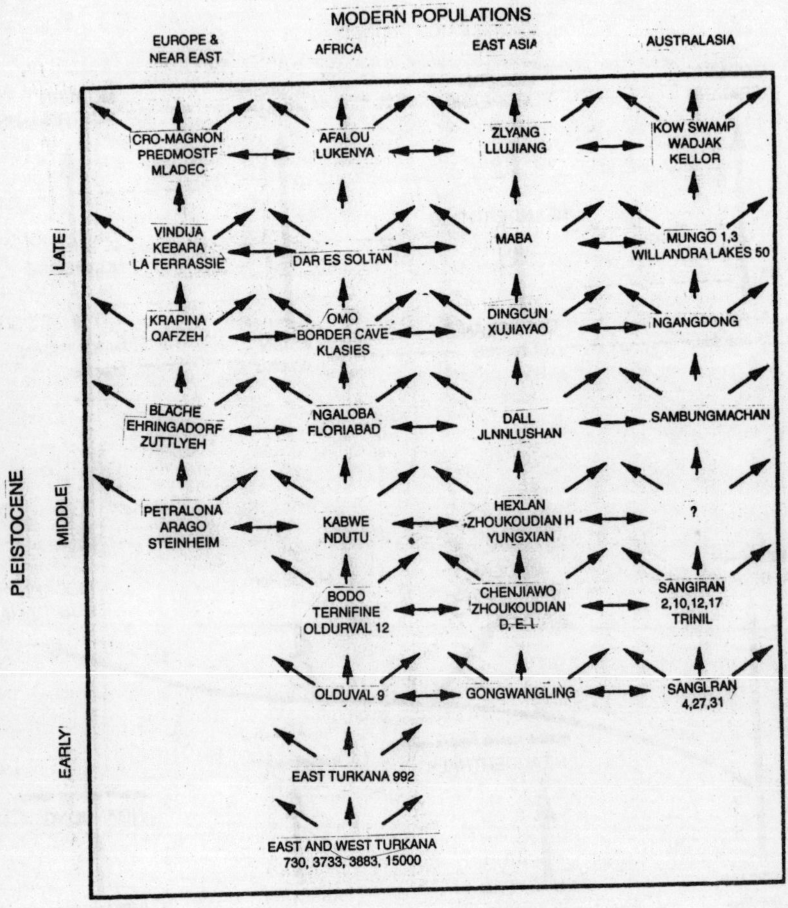

Fig. 5 : The *multiregional* model as elaborated by its supporter.[29] The arrows show the balance condition during the time between the regional continuity (vertical arrows) and the interregional gene flow and/or migration processes (horizontal and diagonal arrows). It is also suggested that selection and genic drift could be more intense (or directional) in the "peripheries" (Europe and Australasia) than in the "centre" (Africa and Asia).

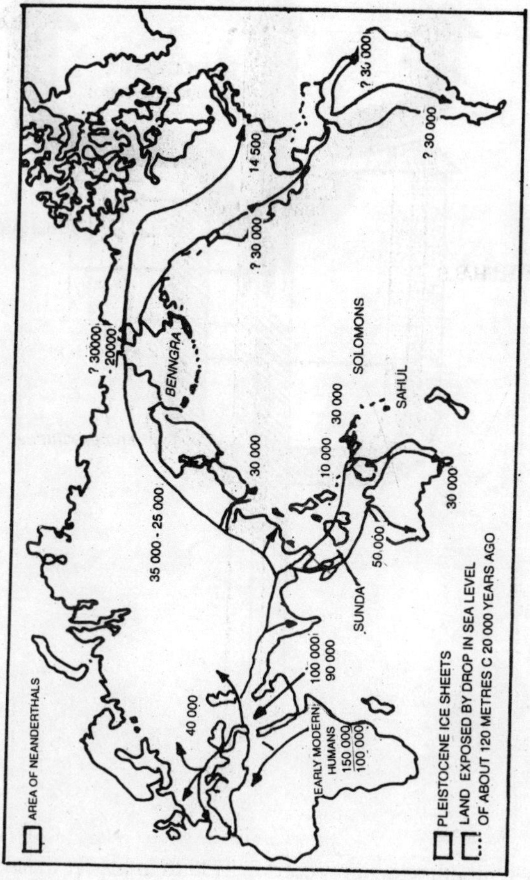

Fig. 6 : Datings and hypothetical routes of a.m. *H. sapiens* diffusion, according to a recent African origin.[47]

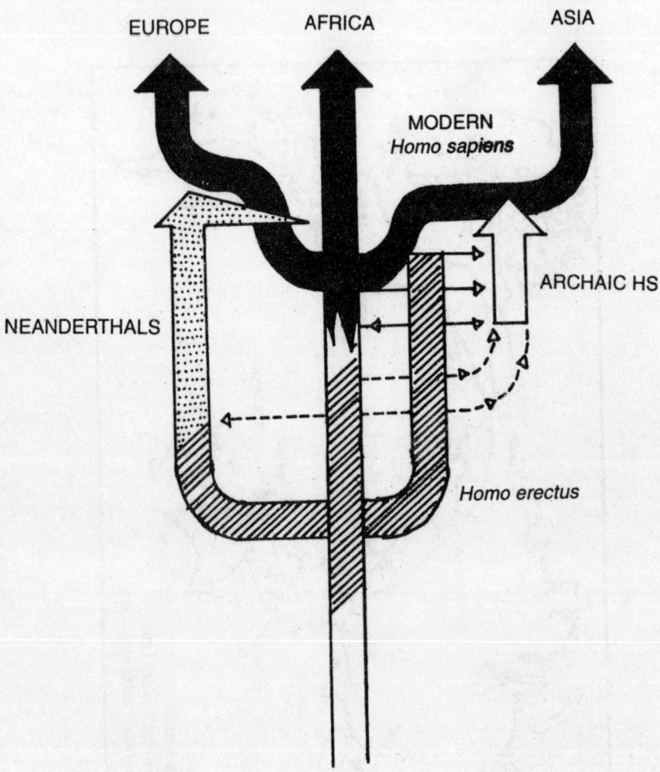

Fig. 7 : A synthetic view proposed in 1993 to interpret the evolution of modern humans in terms of distinct trajectories in the different regions.[35] It can be recognised: The original diffusion of *H. erectus* (sketched); the European evolution of the Neanderthals (dotted) and their diffusion in the Levant; archaic humans in Africa and Asia (white): the African origin and the following diffusion of a.m. *H. sapiens* (black); the gene flow between archaic populations (white arrows) and more modern populations (black arrows).

4

Cosmic, Cultural and Biological Evolutionism

Francesco Barone

The theme of "evolution" seems to appeal once again to popular imagination today, still characterized by the aspects of fascination and heated debate it caused in the past century, during the decades following the Darwinian theory about the origin of animal species. It probably holds an even greater fascination and interest now because today "historical transformation" (which is the essence of the term "evolution") no longer appears as a prerogative of humans, on the basis of a belief dating back to ancient times, but rather of life itself, because as Darwin's contemporaries argued "humans derive from apes" and even from the inorganic universe; in this universe evolution is the motor, while thermodynamic balance is the death.

There are undoubtedly varying degrees of clarity in the awareness people have to cosmic, biological and cultural evolution within a unified evolutionary framework. There is an immediate and experienced sense of the changes in ideas which we express linguistically in our culture, that is in the range of expressions of our materials, social and spiritual life as members of a community and depending on the environmental conditions and the different historic periods.

In our Western tradition the studies on language and society led us, long before Darwin to regard some forms of cultural transmission from one generation to the next as a process of selection as a consequence of which those behaviours prevail and survive that lead to the casual formation of a more efficient order inside the group adopting them. The latter consequently reaches a privileged position in comparison with other groups.

This means that, in spite of the technical difficulties in understanding the genetic and molecular biological processes at the basis of biological evolution, also non-specialists have now become used to considering the history of life from the first prokaryote living three and a half billion years ago up to modern mammals and humans as an evolutionary progress guided by genetic variability, selection and competition, combined with extinction.

These basic theories, on the other hand, led us to a comprehension of the inorganic world and of the universe in general, even though the technical difficulties in understanding the arguments in favour of cosmic evolution are even greater here for non-specialists, that is for most of us. They range from the consequences of the second thermodynamics principle (according to which the transformation of work into heat is not completely reversible), that questions the mechanistic view of physical phenomena and introduces a historical dimension to the subject, to the study of the evolution of stars and the research on distances and spectrums of extragalactic nebulae which led scientists to understand that galaxies move away from us at a speed which is proportional to their distance and independent of their direction.

Over and above technical difficulties, we are now used to extending the concept of evolution beyond life. Earth and stars, to the universe as a whole and finding how it originate the cosmology of *Big Bong*—and to a history which made life possible and, through biological evolution, the life of that particular organism. *Homo sapiens sapiens*, who is able to "observe" the universe, its moments and its components.

This unified evolutionary framework, which today seems to be at the centre of popular imagination, produces at the same time a feeling of fascination and concern.

It is fascinating because this continuity of the evolution process is often interpreted as a continuous progress, following the theories of Herbert Spencer who was the first to describe "evolution" as the opposite of "involution" or "dissolution", five years before *The Origin of Species* (published in 1859), where surprisingly the term "evolution" is not used. It is interesting to note how Spencer himself, in *Progress: Its Law and Cause* states that "it does not matter whether we talk about the development of the Earth or the evolution of life on its surface, the development of society, government, industry, trade, language, literature, science or art, because at the basis of every progress there is the same evolution which moves from simple to complex aspects through subsequent differentiations".

There is no doubt that our century, after the experience of two world wars with devastating effects due to the increasingly powerful destruction weapons used, and thanks to the developments in science and technology, has lost much of the optimistic enthusiasm which led Positivists to sing *paulo maiora canamus* and to think that the "magnificent and progressive fate" of human was becoming close at hand. In spite of all this, the developments in the unified evolutionary framework during the nineteenth century, somehow kept the hope that evolution is a progress towards the better alive and that, as far as *Homo* is concerned, the developments in cultural evolution, especially in the technological field, will open up new chances for Nietzsche's dream of a passage from man to superman. This would happen not so much through the introduction of miniaturized electronic device inside our body (which *cyberpunk* literature likes to fantasize about) as would increase our physical potential, but rather through the improvement of our characteristics as social animals. These features are underlined today by some ethologists who leave in the background aspects such as the aggressiveness of *Homo*, that have been stressed by other ethological studies instead.

A significant instance of this interest of popular imagination for a future superman, especially as a social and moral being, is provided by the title given by one of the weekly supplements designed, not always successfully, by our daily newspapers to boost sales, to an article about evolution which read "You were an ape, you will become an angel". The article is embellished by a beautiful diagram illustrating the various phases of evolution of hominides, on the basis of fossil findings, which have been reconstructed by Palaeontologists today: *Australopithecus afarensis, Australopithecus africanus, Australlopithecus robustus, Homo Abilis, Homo Erectus, Homo Sapiens* (archaic), *Homo sapiens* (*Neanderthalensis*), *Homo sapiens sapiens* (to which we belong as well). The table ends with the sketched drawing of a human figure with angel wings, accompanied by the following comment: "What will become of humans in a million years? Since matter is nothing more than a form of frozen energy, we might become creatures of the light". The article, in perfect agreement with the current rebirth of interest in the study of angels, ends with the significant statement that angels are "our future which makes its comeback".

The increasingly widespread evolutionism, apart from the fascination provided by the more or less explicit optimism it contains, also raises concern in popular imagination, because culture notoriously develops faster than biological evolution. In our century, however, there has been a tremendous acceleration in the speed of this evolution, from the point of view of the scientific-technological dimension of our cultural development, and many people now believe that biological and technological evolution of human beings are intertwined in a "biotechnological" evolution. Contrary to the idea of the creation of a *Homa angelicus* which was mentioned above, we would be moving in the direction of a *Homo technologicus*, a sort of symbiont, to use the definition given by Giuseppe O. Longo, where Darwinian and Lamarckian mechanisms work together, that is casual variations and selection combined with the planning of variation and the transmission from one generation to the next of acquired characteristics. According to current and prevailing scientific interpretations instead, these mechanisms characterize, in an exclusive way, cultural development and biological evolution.

The specificity of the *Homo technologicus* can be understood by considering the technological development which began in the 1970s and goes under the name of "genetic engineering" that is the theoretical study and practical application of controlled modifications which can be introduced in the genetic endowment of living organisms.

It is certainly true that biological evolution on the whole has progressed at random up until at least ten thousand years ago, when our ancestors who can be regarded as the first "biotechnologists" discovered agriculture and animal breeding because they managed to cultivate some plants and tame animals, providing in this way evolution with selective characteristics. However, they did so without being able to interfere with its mechanisms. This is what has become possible for genetic engineers who are able to directly control evolution, by acting on the genetic material and thus carrying out a control which is, or can be finalized, on the substratum of evolution itself.

It is within this framework that the evolutionary perspective has started to cause concern, because the Great Engineer of the forthcoming Republic of Clonia can become even more threatening and dangerous for the future of society and human individuals than the Big Brother described by George Orwell in his novel *1984* at the dawn of the computer revolution. There is the possibility of creating a society structured in the same way as a beehive or an ant-colony, controlled according to the plans of a ruler and dominated by an elite of faithful replicants.

These are not only hallucinations of non-specialists or enemies of science and technology, who are incapable of grasping the relevance these changes have in human culture and their inevitability. One of the founders of molecular biology, Erwin Chargaff in his autobiography complains about two "dangerous discoveries" which have marked his life, namely "atomic fission and the chemical explanation of hereditary factors". In both cases a nucleus was mishandled and, he writes, "I have the impression that science has overstepped a limit which it should have been afraid of".

The modern unified framework of evolutionism carries with it deep-rooted ambiguities which have to be taken into consideration because evolutionism is the perspective from which we look at and tend to interpret the environment we live in as well as ourselves. This paper attempts to clarify these ambiguities, not in order to eliminate them as alleged obstacles to cool rationality, but to better understand their meaning.

From what has been said so far, a first striking ambiguity immediately becomes apparent: is evolutionism a "scientific" or a "philosophical" question? This is probably not so much a matter of "either-or" but rather of "both-and".

Most of the statements about cosmic, biological and cultural evolution are rooted into the research carried out by physicists, biologists and anthropologists: they are characterised by the procedures of documentation, testing and argumentation which are commonly attributed to scientific knowledge, even when the specificity of the individual branches is considered. On the other hand, the "optimistic" or "pessimistic" tinges which have been briefly outlined and could be described at greater length as accompanying the evolutionary hypothesis in popular imagination and, what is even more important, in the minds of scientists themselves, have markedly "subjective" characteristics which belong more to philosophical visions than to scientific "intersubjectivity".

There is an interplay of scientific and philosophical views which the non-specialists "resent" because it often comes up and emerges even in the expressions used by scientists. A significant example of this is provided by the new emergence of the traditional juxtaposition between "mechanicism" and "vitalism" among molecular biologists, even though these scientists agree in characterizing living systems by the existence of a hereditary programme, which results in growth processes and physiological functions. This happens because the self-regulation of the organic "machine" from a conceptual point of view, brings back the famous division between "matter" and "form". The paradoxical proposal, which was not totally meant as a joke, made at the beginning of the 1970s by Max Delbuck—one of the most important representatives of molecular biology—of awarding Aristotle the Nobel Prize for this discipline, is significant in this regard.

By the same token, within the framework of cosmic evolutionism, the debate among cosmologists about the so-called "anthropic principle" is extremely relevant. The division between supporters of its "weaker" version, according to which we are able to effectively observe the existence of a combination between the values of the basic physical constants which is a prerequisite for the formation of the biological tree, only because if these values were different there would be no organism able to observe it, and the supporters of its more "radical" version according to which that combination has certain characteristics so that the corresponding universe is able to accommodate all levels of life up to that of *Homo*, is nothing more than the emergence under an extremely sophisticated technical form of the traditional philosophical contrast between anti-finalism and finalism.

This interplay of scientific and philosophical questions can generate confusion, therefore there have been attempts at making distinctions, possibly using the term "evolution" to define scientific theories, especially those concerning the transformation of living species one into the other, but also the ones concerning the transformation of cosmic conditions and cultural changes. On the other hand the term "evolutionism" has been used to indicate the general trend of these transformations, the direction in which they proceed and the "meaning" of such progress. In this way "evolutionism" becomes a metaphysical theory to explain reality as a whole.

The problem is real, but may be the juxtaposition of the two terms mentioned above, which are used here as synonyms and without being contrasted, is not sufficient to explain it all. The definition given in Popper's autobiography of Darwinism as a "metaphysical research programme" seems appealing, although it might need further commenting and integrating.

When Popper talks about Darwinism he refers to the prevailing doctrine in contemporary biology, which is also known as "neo-Darwinism" or "new synthesis", according to which the various forms of life on earth all belong to one evolutionary tree whose existence is made possible by genetic variation, casual mutations and inheritance. But Popper himself, starting in 1961, insists on the opportunity of integrating this "new synthesis" with a greater attention to orthogenetic trends, that is non-casual evolutionary paths through which evolution leads to forms of life which can be regarded as more complex and "superior". The reason for this is that in those years Popper was working on an evolutionary version of his theory of human knowledge as a solution to the problems through trial and error, leading to a sort of natural selection of hypotheses, even though in the cultural evolution of knowledge there is a trend towards integration within unified theories.

The evolutionary continuity between *Homo* and other animals, even the simplest of species, is taken for granted, but Popper also intends to underline the difference between them. He gives an example, which often comes up in his works, where he says that the greatest difference between Einstein, taken as a model of *Homo* as a talking animal, and an amoeba is that Einstein consciously tries to eliminate the mistakes from his theories, while the amoeba does not have a critical attitude towards its expectations because they are part of it. Humans on the other hand are able to criticize their knowledge and to make it objective by saying what they think, or better by writing it or even by printing it. For this reason, when Popper introduces the concept of "World 3" to indicate the products of human culture, he explicitly states that this world has to be inserted "within an evolutionary theory".

Therefore it seems possible, from Popper's point of view, to talk about "evolutionism" rather than "Darwinism" as a "metaphysical research programme". What meaning, then, does the definition of "metaphysical" with regard to this programme have?

On the basis of the famous distinction made by Popper between science and metaphysics, the statements of the latter cannot be falsified. And given that evolutionism, or Darwinism, do not make forecasts about the evolution phase, nor do they explain them even though they shed light on most concrete research. Popper reaches the conclusion that the statements made by evolutionism cannot be verified and are therefore to be regarded as "metaphysical".

Let's accept this view. But, in the light of what has been said before, evolutionism not only cannot be considered a scientific theory because its basic statements are not verifiable, even though they are useful in formulating verifiable (and therefore scientific) statements about specific theories. It is also "metaphysical" in the sense that the unified picture of the world which is useful for our descriptions is involved in the questions we ask ourselves about the meaning of the world, and not only about its structure.

It is possible to get a clearer view of the interplay within evolutionism, of scientific and philosophical arguments, by assuming that "science" and "philosophy" are not two opposite moments in human culture, as they have often been considered in the tradition of our Western world, but rather two contemporary moments sharing a common existential root.

The indications provided by the cultural evolution of *Homo* show the analogies and also the differences in comparison with animal culture, in the development of which ideas and innovations have the function of genes and mutations in biological evolution and where, unlike the latter, there is a transmission of acquired characters from one generation to the next.

Like other animals, *Homo* survives by adapting to the environment and changing it, thanks to human technological skills, in order to make it as hospitable as possible. But *Homo* also has the original peculiarity of being a talking animal; this verbal language, with its structures affecting also the other human forms of expressiveness and adaptation, makes human beings unique cultural animals.

The constitutional linguistic capacity of *Homo* characterizes first of all the response given by humans to the biological-existential need common to all animals, that of becoming compatible with the environment or perishing. It is indeed through language that we manage to picture the images we have of the things among which we live, in this way we make them objective and they become detached from our immediate way of experiencing them, so that it is possible to coordinate and compare these descriptions. The cultural activity which we call "knowing" derives from this language transcendence of our experiences and it is from the development of this common or "daily" knowledge, which is in itself a cultural answer to the biological-existential question of survival, that what has been defined as "science" by our Western tradition originate. This indicates the whole coordinated, rigorous, generally accepted knowledge which, once applied to the external environment, enables us to act effectively. There is no doubt that what has been from time to time indicated as "episteme", "scientia" and "science" during our cultural evolution from classical antiquity to the present day, has a different aspect, but the thread connecting all these definitions is the pursuit with each of them of the quest for a verifiable and objective knowledge as a cultural answer to the biological-existential need of understanding how things are in order to become compatible with them and survive. We need to have an "image of the world", of which we feel the "hardship".

Homo too, however, like other animals—especially the ones which have been tamed and with which we have some familiarity

—apart from "feeling" the world through senses, is "affected" by it emotionally, because humans feel attraction or repulsion, desires, wishes, fears. Their biological-existential need of understanding how things are always accompanied by the need of taking an attitude and a stand, almost in a passionate way, towards them.

Here again, our linguistic specificity as cultural animals allows us to describe our emotional attitudes, to make them objective in terms of value, in the same way as our linguistic capacity allows us to make them objective, by describing them, our images of things. Typical of *Homo* in this cultural moment is the emergence inside humans of a "sense of death" as a consequence of which, regardless of the image of the world we have, this is always accompanied by the disappointment for the inevitable end threatening us, the dreaded question about the sense of death and our transitory existence.

It is within this existential question that the cultural moment which in our tradition takes the name of "philosophy" or "metaphysics" originates in the most widespread meaning given to these terms. But, regardless of the names attributed to them by other cultural traditions, in the cultural evolution of *Homo* there are always these two moments deriving from the joint biological-existential need of creating an image of the world we live in and of making sense out of our existence inside it; in our tradition this quest has found an answer with the development of "science" and "philosophy".

It is, therefore, hardly surprising that there should be an interplay of scientific and philosophical questions within "evolutionism", the latter is undoubtedly an "image of the world" which has been constructed during cultural evolution through refined research on that knowledge which is coordinated, controlled and generally accepted and goes under the name of "science". However, like any other more or less refined "image of the world", this one too cannot be separated and radically unrooted from its existential unity with a "view of the world", which means giving an axiological significance to everything (including ourselves) that belongs to the image. Every *Weltbild* can be distinguished but not separated from a *Weltanschauung*. In fact it is possible to distinguish the ontological-gnoseological beliefs which make up an "image of the world" from the axiological (sense-giving) characteristics typical of the "view of the world" which the image belongs to. Indeed, similar images of the world can be found in different world views, but the fact remains that the combination *Weltbild-Weltanschauung* is inseparable for *Homo.*

There are also other reasons which lead to regard evolutionism as a *Weltbild* inevitably connected with some sort of *Weltanschauung* rather than with a "metaphysical research programme" as Popper said.

The current success of the evolutionary image of the world can be explained in various ways. First of all it is a strong image which unifies knowledge in a variety of fields, from cosmology to physics, from biology to anthropology. There is no denying that the ambition to unify knowledge is typical of science and it is difficult to find in other images of the world, important as they may have been for scientific evolution, the same unifying capacity. Think, for example, of the image of the world as an organism, typical of Aristotle and peripatetic science as for a long time it has been opposed to introducing a mathematical interpretation of physical phenomena which is typical of modern physics. By the same token, the new image of the world as a clock, imposed by modern physics itself, in spite of its success in the individual sectors, has sometimes hindered the research into so-called "Baconian", that is, non-mathematical sciences. Evolutionism, on the other hand, stresses the historical dimension of reality, unifies and does not contrast the various fields of research.

There is another question worth mentioning. While the cultural evolution of the *Weltbild* has given rise to increasing specialization through scientific research, the cultural evolution of the *Weltanschauung* has preserved some of its peculiarities in the "philosophies". The axiological character of sense-making certainly increases the subjective features of philosophical answers, because the greatest concern of all individuals is always the problems of their "own" transience and end. But within the limitless range of subjective tinges there are always two standard answers: the "mundane" and the "extramundane", or, to use a plastic Platonic metaphor, the one given by the "Children of the Earth" and the one given by the "Friends of Forms".

In the whole cultural history of the *Weltanschamungen* there emerges, in a wide variety of forms, the attempt at making sense of the same world we live in and of which we create an image for ourselves, or the opposite attempt at making sense of this world through another world or another project which goes beyond and creates it. This is a dichotomy which cannot be mediated: one can argue in favour of one or the other option to make it appear more plausible, but these arguments are different from those through which, on a scientific level, people try to control the images of the world intersubjectively. In both kinds of *Weltanschauung* an "irrational" faith is at work compared to scientific methods: it is an irrational faith in reason or in what transcends reason.

This also explains why the elaboration of the evolutionary view of the world, which has been gaining ground during the past century, is accompanied by a continuous shift between a mundane and an extramundane vision, between a mechanistic-reductionist and a finalistic vision, where not even the most refined transcription of that image into scientific theories, carefully controlled and containing a wealth of explanations for every phenomenon, has been able to "demonstrate" beyond doubt that one "view" or the other is wrong. The truth is that each of those transcripts and the corresponding scientific theories is always formulated, more or less explicitly, in view of one vision or the other.

This clearly appears in the case of social Darwinism on the one side and the telefinalism of the immunologist Le Comte de Nouy or the idea of the omega principle of the paleontologist Teilhard de Chardin on the other. But it is always present, even though not in such an apparent way, in all the biological research about evolutionary phenomena which still questions the neo-Lamarckian or the neo-Darwinian orientation, in spite of the fact that the concept of non-inheritance of acquired characters in the biological field has now been solved in favour of the latter.

More than sixty years ago, Caullery, in his book about biology entitled *Probleme de I' Evolution*, wrote that "The fact of evolution is unquestionable, only its mechanism is uncertain". Now, after decades of strongly innovative research and results. Caullery's conclusion on the whole still remains valid, just think of the fossil findings and their dating through radiometric methods, the studies on inheritance, and the research on molecular biology which allow us to reconstruct the changes which have taken place over time in certain molecules and the corresponding structural changes inside the organisms. Once the idea of evolution as a scientific phenomenon has been accepted, the debate about the mechanisms of evolution, about how and why a certain evolutionary process takes place, remains open.

The situation is particularly stimulating from an epistemological point of view, because it provides unique indications about the ways in which that *Weltbild*, which is originally a cultural answer to a biological-existential need of *Homo*, develops from a scientific point of view. The result of scientific knowledge is the formulation of theories which can be empirically tested to explain certain phenomena, but there is no single method of formulating these theories even if we admit that they can be considered scientific because they can be tested empirically. The explanatory theories are hypotheses and one of the elements at the basis of the hypothesis is the kind of *Weltanschauung* to which the *Weltbild* originating scientific knowledge belongs. This trend originates "programmes" or "research traditions" with specific characteristics, within which the individual scientific theories aimed at explaining, in a controlled way, certain phenomena are inserted.

Examples of "research traditions" characterized by metaphysical features are, for instance, in nineteenth century physics, mechanicism and energetism, within which rival theories develop: just think of mechanicism, the kinetic theory of matter which Lord Kelvin (albeit not very successfully) tried to oppose to the theories elaborated by Clausius, Maxwell and Boltzmann. Both these theories shared an "atomic" vision of physical reality which, on the other hand, was rejected by the energetist vision of the world.

Similar examples of analogous research traditions with metaphysical features are at the basis of specific scientific research which studies evolution in its various forms, from the universe to human beings. Each of these research areas, as it is carried out concretely, thinks that it must answer only to those intersubjectivity and verifiability criteria which at a given time appear essential for that discipline. But these research areas are different because they are rooted into research traditions which, even though they share the same evolutionary *Weltbild*, are placed inside opposite "views of the world". For evolution in general we have seen that these are the mechanistic and finalistic views, even though mechanicism here does not correspond with the explanatory models of traditional physics, nor does finalism only mean conscious elaboration of a project, but also subconscious orientations. For biological evolution, especially these views take the form of "neo-Darwinism" and "neo-Lamarckism" that is the thesis maintaining the mere casuality of genetic mutation, or the acknowledgement of a tendency of the organism to take in the environmental stimuli.

In our century, neo-Darwinism has been the dominant research tradition for the formulation of scientific theories to explain evolutionary processes. But today some of those mechanisms seem difficult to explain on the basis of traditional neo-Darwinian theories. We have already seen how Popper underlined such difficulties in explaining the phenomena of orthogenesis; similarly relevant difficulties arise for the synthetic theory, based on a gradual evolution of the species, from paleontological research testifying to sudden changes and long static periods. And interesting controversies about traditional explanations also derive from discoveries of molecular biology concerning the distinction between different classes of genes, those whose task it is to produce material and those which regulate production.

This means that the proud statement, often repeated, that neo-Darwinism has now "defeated" neo-Lamarckism and the like, today looks more like the expression of a metaphysical ambition rather than the declaration of a truth. Interestingly enough, in an article published by *Le Scienze* in November, 1994, Marvin Minsky wrote about the ideas which biologists call "teleological" and "Lamarckian", saying that "it has taken more than a century for evolutionists to get rid of them, but today they may be forced to change the rules once again".

It is not surprising, when talking about evolution, that there have been changes even in the scientific explanation of evolutionary phenomena and in the choice of the relevant "research traditions".

5

The Bronze Age Barrows in Denmark

Jens Poulsen

A typical burial mound from the Bronze Age in Denmark is at least two metres high and on average fifteen to twenty metres in diameter, but many barrows are considerably bigger. Of such Bronze Age barrows, in Denmark a recorded knowledge of a number close to 20,000 is the Archival studies make it likely that they represent about at least half, perhaps even only a third, of the barrows originally constructed in the Bronze Age, i.e., some 40,000 to 60,000 in total.

How do the barrows also called burial mounds, come into this picture? It is well known that to the plough farmer the barrows represent an obstacle to efficient agriculture. As far as possible the farmer therefore removes the barrows to get an even ground surface over an extended area of land. In many parts of Europe, as also in Denmark, systematic destruction and clearance of prehistoric barrows has been carried out especially during the last 200 years. This has regularly been the case on land owned by the nobility and on other large estates where an intensified grain cultivation was wanted in order to increase the income. However, ordinary common farmers have certainly contributed to the general destruction too.

It is characteristic that this destruction of barrows relates, of course, mostly to land with the good and fertile clayey soils which bring the biggest economic surplus to agriculture. Hence, of the still preserved burial mounds in Europe, the majority tends to be present on the less fertile sandy or gravel soils while only a minority, if any at all, are present on the more fertile clayey soils. Denmark, which abounds in such sites, is a country well suited for the archaeological study of this subject.

Surprisingly, many of the recorded barrows are well preserved, while others have been ploughed but are still recognizable to the trained eye. It must be called a miracle that such an impressive number has survived the intensive plough farming which has taken place since the nineteenth century before legislation brought the destruction of barrows to a halt. It is complicated to explain the miracle, but it may have to do with the original number of mounds ever constructed in prehistory. So it goes without gainsaying that the more barrows that are still visible in a country, the greater the original total number of barrows is likely to have been. It should be mentioned that apart from the barrows from the Bronze Age, thousands of burial mounds dating to the Neolithic Age are also still preserved in Denmark.

The study of the Bronze Age in Denmark is based on three categories of finds—the burials, the hoards/votive offerings and the habitation sites. Compared to the other categories, the burials make up the predominant category. This is due to their sheer numbers and to the generally quite informative finds which have been found in the limited proportion of the barrows which have been excavated.

It is highly likely that the large majority of the many thousands of barrows from the Bronze Age were constructed during the greater part of its first half, that is, in Periods II to III or 1500-1000 BC, when the tradition of inhumation prevailed. They were normally in use also during the Late Bronze Age or 1000-500 BC when the custom of cremation was total, sometimes even during the following pre-Roman Iron Age.

What kind of information can be obtained from the excavation and other investigations of burial mounds that can contribute to the reconstruction of the Bronze Age society in Denmark? They tell us about their own construction and that of the burials inside them, about the way the dead corpses were prepared for burial, e.g. whether they were inhumed or cremated, and how the dead persons were provided for in their after-life. This gives us an insight into the organization of the general society and of the local community and sometimes also into the relations with other communities in the region as well as those abroad. Finally, the distribution of the mounds in the landscape yields important information about settlement patterns and communication lines.

The mounds consist of earth, but it appears that they were not build by just piling loads of loose earth on top of each other. Rather they were constructed using standard sized turfs or heath peat carefully arranged to make the bulk of the mound as solid as possible. A circle of stones was regularly set up around the foot of the mound to support the earth fill of it, but often evidently also to increase the monumentality of the mound. Excavations show that in the course of time when new burials were to take place at a mound site, it was normal to enlarge the mounds both in height and in width and also to erect new and larger stone circles around the new mound foot. The stratigraphic study of these construction phases and the relation of the individual burials to them is crucial for the interpretation of the mounds as burial places, but also of course as regards general chronological questions. The burial mounds of the Early Bronze Age occur either singly or in small groups, and the favoured location of them was at the top of hills or ranges making them visible at a distance. Today the mounds from the Bronze Age make up a very characteristic feature of the countryside in many parts of Denmark.

For the construction of the graves wood or stone was used. The two to three metres long oak coffins are especially interesting. They are made out of either halved or hollowed out trunks of oak. Various complicated chemical and physical conditions for the preservation of organic matter of the earth mounds as a whole mean that not only have many of these wooden coffins themselves survived in fine form, but also the ox hide wrapped around the inhumed corpse, the well dressed hair and the woven woollen textile dresses of the buried person inside them. These woollen dresses are exceptionally well preserved in their entirety and are without parallel in contemporary Bronze Age Europe. Their contribution to the study of the history of the art of weaving and dress making in Europe is unique.

Numerous excavated graves have yielded information about

the grave goods of bronze and gold given to the persons buried in them that is extremely important for the study of the social organization of the Bronze Age communities. The craftsmanship and quality, style and beauty of these Nordic bronze and gold artefacts make this region of Europe quite outstanding in the Bronze Age. Men were equipped with their weapons such as swords, daggers, spears and axes, working tools such as axes and chisels, as well as razors and tweezers and personal ornaments and sometimes also imported metal objects of a luxury character. Women were provided with their personal ornaments and sometimes also with tools and even weapons such as daggers. Only very few children's graves have been recorded, but it is only as an exception that they contain grave goods, sometimes of such a value that the buried children probably belonged to high ranking families.

From the point of view of the original total populations of the local communities, the large majority was apparently not buried in the mounds, but in all likelihood outside them under flat grounds. The mounds as special burial places were mostly reserved for persons of high ranking families, and interestingly the female members allowed a mound burial were far outnumbered by the male members. The general rule was one female member for each two to three male members of the chiefly groups of the society. This tradition varies a lot locally in terms of increased outnumbering of female by male burials. In spite of the fact of this tradition, women have quite often been buried with rich grave goods, sometimes including even objects of gold, a material normally reserved for artefacts belonging to men.

The number and quality of the bronze and gold artefacts found in the graves is very variable in both male and female graves, and these customs also vary locally. In short, there is a vast quantity of material available for studies of the social differentiation within the chiefly section of the society. The basis for this type of society in Denmark and the rest of southern Scandinavia was the complex business of trading metals from central Europe—possibly for amber collected along the sea shores and for furs from the northern parts of the Scandinavian peninsula.

Settlement archaeology is currently one of the central subjects in archaeology. The best type of evidence of course is habitation sites, but where they are too few or ill-dated the attention must be drawn to other types of sites. This is the case in Denmark where studies of the settlement in the Bronze Age must make use of the evidence provided by the burials because it is many hundred times bigger than that of the very sites where people lived and from which they farmed their land.

Some more careful excavations show that the burial mounds containing the burials were sometimes constructed on the ground surface of farmed land or of habitation sites having apparently just been given up. The very rare more closely datable habitation sites are sometimes situated near mounds that were used for burial in the same period. The burial mounds thus represent the settled land in the Bronze Age. As a find category they therefore supply important information about the development of the settlement. Since the large majority of the mounds from the Early Bronze Age dates to the 500 years covering Periods II and III, it is interesting to observe the character of settlements during that period of time.

A few basic questions to throw light on this important subject may turn up like how often was the individual barrow that was used for burial in Period II in fact used for this purpose again in Period III and how often was a particular barrow used only in Period III. The literature leaves the impression that the mounds were used for burial continuously throughout these two periods. But, in fact, strangely enough these simple and obvious questions have never been really asked and investigated. Whatever the answer, they will tell us something about the character of the settlement and of the agricultural technology and their development in the course of the 500 years concerned. The matter may be illustrated by its two extremes that if people regularly used the same mounds for burials continuously during both these two periods, then the settlement is likely to have been of a correspondingly permanent or stable character or, to put it simply, the people did not move their farms and homes very far. If, on the other hand, people never or only rarely used the same mounds in more than one period, the settlement is likely to have been of a correspondingly labile or fluctuating character, i.e., the people moved to other places at some distance from the old ones.

I am presently examining this matter in the Danish material and shall very briefly outline the result for the southern part of the Jutland peninsula. Figure 1 is thought to be representative of Denmark as a whole. Figure 2 shows that the chronological pattern is quite different from the traditional view. Burials were only very exceptionally made in the same mounds in both Period II and Period III. The normal practice was thus to use different mounds in each period. The spatial relationship between the filled circles = Period II barrows, and the filled triangles = Period III barrows, illustrates that there is no uniform developmental pattern in the course of Period II and Period III. In some places the settlement remained in the same area but contracted or expanded in contact with the old core, while in other places it took up new, hitherto, unsettled areas at some distance away from the previously settled home areas, a change that seems to reflect a kind of small scale internal colonization. The unexpectedly rare mounds used in both periods (cf. the filled quadrangles) are located in places with a dense distribution of mounds.

These observations are interpreted in terms of subsistence economy and population size. Without being forced to do so, presumably no farmer would leave a place well suited for agricultural production. In case of need for larger areas for the usual types of production or for other, possibly quite new types of production, it would be natural for a growing population just to expand from the core of existing settlement and keep in close contact. Only in situations where such action is held to be impossible or inadequate would it be necessary to move away to quite new places or areas. As the map shows, the nature of the settlement in the Early Bronze Age in Denmark was one of applying both strategies characterized as it was by local variation in terms of permanency/stability as well as by expansion/mobility in the course of the 500-years-long time span concerned.

Careful consideration of this very complicated matter has shown, however, that the distribution and chronology of the Bronze Age mounds are unlikely to be better explained with reference to factors of the destruction of the mounds in modern times than to the realities of the Bronze Age.

Fig. 1: A map of Denmark with the study area in Jutland hatched.

South Jutland, Denmark								
Group		*1*			*2*		*SUM*	*3*
Period	*I*	*II*	*III*	*I-II*	*II-III*	*I-III*		*Period?*
Number	14	175	203	1	18	2	413	91
Percentage	3.4	42.4	49.2	0.2	4.4	0.5		22.0

Group 1: Burial mounds with dated graves from only one period.
Group 2: Burial mounds with dated graves from two or three periods.
Group 3: Burial mounds like (1) and (2), but with other graves from the Early Bronze Age that are not further datable.

Fig. 2: A table of the datable and located burial mounds from the Early Bronze Age in five counties of Jutland in Denmark.

6

Teaching and Training Archaeology at Tomar in Portugal

Luiz Oosterbeek

Iberia is formed by three main geomorphological units: the ancient massif of Precambrian and Cambrian rocks that constitutes the heart and the majority of the peninsula (schist, granite, quartzite) and has continuity with continental Europe and some Atlantic islands near the Portuguese shore; the abraded and flattened limestone surfaces of Secondary and early Tertiary age that define typical Mediterranean landscapes surrounding the former unit: and the Ceno-Anthropozoic basins (like the Tagus) filled with sedimentary deposits. The Mediterranean and the climate, and were also responsible for a very irregular shoreline (today it is fairly regular, but in the Middle Ages it consisted of a complex sequence of bays). The central massif, the Mezeta, also generates continental influences which are evident in the climate which is very dry and with high temperatures in the summer contrasting with sub-zero temperatures in the winter. The variability, in a relatively small area which is almost detached from the rest of Europe and surrounded by water, was historically one of the reasons for the success of the Iberian states in the fifteenth century.

The contrasts are not only between inland and coastal areas. The west, south of the Mondego valley, has no real mountains in most of its length, and it is doubtful if the opposition of highland

and lowland has any meaning in the Alentejo. The evergreen Mediterranean forest of the south contrasts with a major component of deciduous forest in the north.

There is little doubt about the Iberian-Mediterranean interaction, regardless of the models suggested to explain it. Relations with the Atlantic become clear in the third millennium, but it is arguable that they may date from earlier times (megaliths, isolated occurrence of cardial impressed pottery in the French Atlantic shore).

If one considers the main currents between the Iberian and the Italian peninsula, one must consider basically three: from Liguria to Iberia along the coast, turning to the Maghreb in eastern Andalucia; from the Spanish Levante to the Balearics, and then to Sardinia and Corsica; from the Maghreb to Tunisia and Sicily where it splits into two, one heading to southern Italy, and the other to the Eastern Mediterranean.

The Portuguese Atlantic coast is dominated by a northern current, part of which penetrates the Mediterranean through Gibraltar, while the main current follows the North African Atlantic shore.

Iberia shares most of its features with the Mediterranean. A thin plain shore is rapidly broken by chains of mountains, usually calcareous, generating two oppositions, lowland and uplands, and coastal and inland. The rivers are the main natural routes that enable the crossing of these mountains, of which the Tagus, the Mondego, the Guardiana, the Sado and the Guadalquivir will be mentioned often.

The mountains are poor especially due to the very hard, cold and wet winters, and tend to be more conservative. Pastoralism tends to be the main activity, but they also have very good soils for agriculture, like the high plateau valleys. The limestones hill soils also have a lighter texture, which combined with good sun exposure and proper irrigation could support cereal growing very well. Among other measures, both irrigation (in Andalucia) and terracing (in Israel) date at least from the Chalcolithic period.

Terracing, in particular, does not involve too large human groups, and prevents soil erosion while expanding the arable surface, smoothing the slopes and keeping the moisture. The single clear evidence for terracing comes from the Ghassulian period, in the 4th millennium, but indirect evidence has been noted in Greece and Sicily, and examples of Neolithic field systems are known elsewhere. The terraces in the *Casais Novos* area (Nabao valley, Tomar) are also associated with Neolithic artifacts, but unfortunately with no clear stratigraphic relation. Hence, in the early stages of the Neolithic process, hills could have been at least as attractive as the coastal lands, providing a diversified landscape, natural shelters and refuges (caves) and the best access to the lowlands and the mountains.

The plains are more productive, but also more unstable, due to the occurrence of marshes (focus of diseases, and the formation of which is accelerated by deforestation) and floods (still now a major problem in Portugal and, in particular, in the Ribatejo). Their occupation implied probably from the earliest times, some sort of means of control of the abundance from their possible symbolic meaning. It is impossible not to see in them artificial islands for population refuge in case of flood. In fact, these sites integrate both burials and habitation structures, but it is likely that these ones correspond with the flood periods.

As Braudel considers, the occupation of the plains implies much more coordinated and heavy work, and this may be one of the reasons why the earliest Neolithic permanent sites tended to avoid these areas, even if it is a fact that sedentism is clearly associated with the occupation of high arable potential soils in the Western Mediterranean. Even in later periods, settlements need not coincide with these soils since the best location is a central one, and hilltop sites had at least two advantages that access to different types of soils and other resources and location above flood. This was also a reason for the continuous use of caves, which is still in practice in some areas like Andalucia, and constitutes 3 to 7 per cent in some regions of Italy. The rarity of open air settlements in the Neolithic is not due to a real disoccupation though. Erosion has heavily destroyed the original soils and many of the habitation sites in them.

Seasonal transhumane was, any way, a widespread model in the Mediterranean, and it remains a strong possibility for the prehistoric populations in Iberia. Trade, on the other hand, became more and more an important activity. Medieval records show that Andalucian snow was traded to Oran. But it is obvious that the main trade involved food, and this became possible with the combination of transportation (animal traction), storage and in particular conservation (salt) improvements. There is no clear evidence for the use of salt in the Neolithic, but I would argue that it may not be an accident that one of the most important concentrations of Neolithic sites, Rio Maior, also corresponds with the major concentrations of salt in Portugal. It should be noted that a shell midden was found, dating to as early as the ninth millennium, more than 80 km from the coast near Fatima.

Finally, if one considers the mining resource, the West of Iberia is clearly the richest part of the peninsula. Apart from alluvial gold (particularly in the north, but also occurring in other regions), there are important sources of tin (in the north) and copper (in the south). This distribution has been considered when studying early metallurgy, as a support for the "colonies theory" (applied to the fortified Chalocolithic enclosures of Iberia, such as *Los Millares*) or for the "passage" and trade character of central Portugal.

From the point of view of the available archaeological data, central-western Portugal (provinces of Ribatejo and Estremadura) from the Tagus Valley to the Atlantic has been focus of numerous field researches. It has been argued that it constitutes a region in itself. The role played by the Tagus river has also been proved for very early period. The diversity could not be better defined as in the North Ribatejo, where these three geomorphological units meet.

Regions themselves are difficult units to define. All one can do, at first, is to establish environmental units. Some major difficulties arise from such an approach, though. On the one hand, human societies do not confine themselves to any "natural" boundaries, and the purpose of this research is to study human societies. A chain of mountains may be a natural frontier, but it may also be a complementary environment within a transhumane economic model, and therefore a privileged area for human communities interaction. The same goes for a main river. On the other hand, continuous units, like plains of good arable soils, could be "no man's land" for non-agricultural human groups, and therefore an effective socio-spacial limit.

Ecological boundaries are also difficult to establish. This is true for the present, but as has been sufficiently stressed by the paleoeconomists, it is even more significant for past societies. Of the three main variables that compose the environment (apart from humans), one has a limited knowledge of the geomorphology (including pedogenesis), some evidence for the animal and vegetational cover (from their archaeological remains) and barely nothing detailed of the climate. This knowledge is acceptable at larger scales, but it does not apply to particular regions.

The Alto Ribatejo ("North Ribatejo") region itself has no precise boundaries, only gravitational axes. These are considered to be the mid-low Tagus valley and its tributary rivers, the Zezere, with the Nabao: Almonda. It is also a heterogeneous region as it is basically the crossroad of the Mesocenozoic occidental fringe with the Miocene Tagus basin and the Central-Iberian zone of the Ancient Massif, the "Mezeta".

A first approach to site distributions indicated some correlation with the units mentioned, and was recently discussed in an extensive way. The purpose of the project is to assert what the economic potential resources might have been and which of these have actually been used at different stages. The north of Ribatejo Province is presently considered as predominantly industrial, in contrast with the south (Leziria). This is due to an almost total lack of plains in the north, as well as of high arable potential soils such as flood areas. The north has been the location of interior but limited agriculture, and its importance in the Middle Ages and in the industrial revolution derived mainly from its strategic location, due to the different accesses mentioned above, its forest and its good fluvial branches mainly used for early industrial energy supply and good trade.

The geomorphological units associate Mesozoic limestones in the north west (Triasic, Jurassic, Cretaceous and Liassic), Precambrian and Palaeozoic rocks in the north-east, and Ceno-Anthropozoic deposits in the south (Miocene, Plio-Quarternary, Holocene) though the Anthropozoic ones also occur in the top of the other major units. The Pleistocene sequence includes a series of terraces below 100 m, some with middle and upper Palaeolithic remains. The Mesozoic complex is particularly disturbed by many inverse faults, mainly in a north/south direction.

The lithology of these units also includes three main sedimentary complexes: limestones (with flint) in the north-west, sand and sandstone in the south, and schists and granites in the north-east. Plio-Pleistocene quartz and quartzite pebbles occur on top of all these units. Deep alluvium deposits dominate the south, but they also occur in the more shallow valleys of the other two units. The *ph* of soils runs from alkaline in the north-west to medium acidity in the north-east and south.

The region is crossed by two main rivers (Tagus and Zezere), another important fluvial valley, the Nabao, and many smaller rivers and streams, especially in the west, draining the karstic relief of the limestone massif. Natural fresh water springs are numerous, and archaeological sites are often close to either or both of these sources of water.

The agricultural potential of the soils is very good, if one takes the region as a whole, because of its diversity. Basically, the north is good for forestry (classified as class F), and the south has very high potential arable soils (class A). There are some details, though, that might be very important in order to understand the actual soil potential in prehistoric times. First, the northern region does have alluvium deposits, which in spite of being very shallow provide excellent conditions for horticulture. The alkaline soils also have good conditions for nitrification and calcium assimilation, and their main problem is the slow mineralization of organic remains which can be overcome by organic manure. Third, alkaline soils, even without fertilization, do support cereal cultivation and they have the advantage of being light, and therefore easy to work with stone or wood implements. Fourth, the southern soils present two disadvantages, that is, the processes of humidification and nitrification are more difficult, and to overcome this, chemical fertilization is required in the long run, and also they are heavy clayish soils, virtually impossible to use without metal instruments and/or animal traction.

Modern agricultural systems provide some indications. The alluvium soils are considered as being the good ones for agriculture, but they are devoted to extensive mechanical ploughing. The north-eastern soils are mainly used for forestry and pasture, and the north-western ones for forestry alone. Nevertheless, small scale intensive agriculture was current in the area until 30 years ago. Older people (over 60 years) those who still live in the region, keep on developing farming in these light soils which tend to be abandoned by the younger people who migrate to the towns for financial and cultural reasons. But the light northern soils do provide crops on a subsistence basis economy, and are comparatively easy to work on.

Small farmers in the south experience a much harder way of life when they cannot afford to use machines, and hand ploughing of 100 sqm takes about 30 hours of work.

Finally, one must consider that erosion may have been very strong and that the soils on the top of the hills might have been thicker than they are now. Cultivation in the mountainous north therefore presented only one main problem which is the need either to be confined to thin alluvium in the valley, or to develop a terracing system on the slopes, which, of course, implied a certain degree of social coordination. But the use of the wide southern soils could also only be made through the development of irrigation systems, the maintenance of which would certainly imply more continuous communal work.

If one considers the surface lithic remains that can be found by survey, they are concentrated, for the Neolithic, in the north rather than in the north-east or the south. One can therefore assume that it is likely that only in a later period did southern soils begin to be used, at least intensively, as shall be discussed later. Palaeolithic remains are concentrated mainly in the Tagus valley, in imprecise depositional conditions, whereas the north-east of the region seems to have been occupied only in the Late Bronze Age in association with pastoralism and, later, iron extraction.

Climate and biome are even more difficult to assess for prehistoric times. Nevertheless, some major trends that might have been operational in the Atlantic and sub-Boreal periods are indicated. The vegetation cover, today, is roughly Atlantic-Mediterranean, with stronger Mediterranean influence in the south which is natural. The dominant species are *Pinus pinastra atlantic,*

Pinus pinca, Quercus rotundifolia, Olea europea europea and unfortunately increasing *Eucalyptus* spp. Other highly represented species are the *Quercus faginea, Ficus carica, Vitis vinifera vinifera* and fruit trees. *Pinus* is in "recession" and this has been made more serious by recent fire. But it is perhaps more significant, for my purpose, to indicate that many *Quercus rotundifolia* are not cultivated, and that abandoned former agricultural soils tend to be occupied by bushes of *Quercus* spp., thus indicating the potential prevailing original Holocene forestry which might include a more significant percentage of *Quercus faginea*. Cabbage, potatoes and tomatoes are cultivated on a small scale almost everywhere. Two main cereals cultivated are *Zea mays, L.* in the south and *Honleum sativa*. Less in the north has been occasionally associated with *Triticum aestivum*, L.

As has been mentioned, there are no regional paleoecological studies. For the Holocene, it is possible to draw some guidelines from regional models developed for south west Europe, and isolated pollen diagrams obtained for Portugal. Studies in the French Midi revealed a progressive substitution of *Pinus* spp. by *Quercus* spp. throughout the Boreal and Atlantic periods. *Quercus suber* being the dominant species by 5000 BC in the Languedoc. In the Provence region, there was a balance between unforested periods and others dominated by an association of *Quercus* spp. and *Pinus halepensis*, the latter one still being present in the region we are concerned with, and a later dominance of *Quercus rotundifolia* due to man-made influences on the vegetation cover. In spite of the dangers of such long distance parallels, it is likely that *Quercus* spp. and possibly *rotundifolia*, was the dominant species from the third millennium onwards, if one also considers the "spontaneous" vegetation that is currently reoccupying the abandoned former agricultural areas.

The closest pollen diagrams available that are of some interest for this region are from Alpiarca, some 50 km to the south, in the Tagus Valley. The diagrams have been obtained from stratigraphical profiles in the flood plain from a settlement site called *Cabeco da Bruxa*. What these diagrams confirm is both the prevailing presence of *Quercus* spp. and very significantly, an important deforestation in the last third millennium. This evidence is surely very important, since it matches the assumptions I have been making for the use of the southern soils of North Ribatejo (that are the extreme north of the flood plain—Leziria—deposits, where Alpiarca stands). It also clearly indicates a later deposition than in the Central Massif "Serra da Estrela", the highest mountain of Portugal, where evidence of intensive use of soils has been dated back to the fifth millennium, in an area over 1500 m above sea-level, and with very poor agricultural potential, to our present standard.

It is in this region that the research of the Laboratory of Prehistory and the Landscape Archaeology research degree of Tomar follow their activities. Relevant issues, such as the *Languedocian* technocomplex, or the colonization versus acculturation of the Iberian communities at different stages, are the main questions suggested for international research.

REFERENCES

1985, 'A Gruta do Cadaval: Elementos para a Pre-Historia do Vale do Nabao', *Arqueologia na Regiao de Toma*, Vol 1, 61-76

1993, Artes Tradicionais: a ceramica: Contributo para una metado logia de analse te chomorfologica, *Bdetein Cultural la Camara Municipal de Tomar*, Vol. 19

Cruz, A.R., 1989, *Pre Historia: Do campo ao iaboratorio.*

Tomar: Escok Superior de Technologia de Tomar

Drewett, P., L. Oosterbeek, A.R. Cruz, P. Felix, 1992, Anta 1 de Val da Laje 1989/90 - The excavation of a passage grave at Tomar (Portugal). *Bulletin of the Institute of Archaeology*, London.

Oosterbeek, L. 1985: Elementos para o estudo da Estratigrafia da Gruta do Cadaval (Tomar). Almadan, vol. 4/5: 7-12.

———, 1987: Projecto de Estudo da Neolitizacao do Vale do Nabao, A Gestao dos Espacos e os Metodos de Abordagem, IN: A.P. Manique. Temas de Historia do Distrito de Santarem. Santarem, Escola Superior de Educacao de Santarem.

———, 1988: Para a revisao da Neolitizacao da regiao de Torres Novas. ALmondinha, vol. 1: 10-12.

L. Oosterbeek, Cruz, A.R., 1985, 'Gruta do Cadaval - 1983' in *Informacao arqueologica*, Vols., 117-8

———, 1988: Neolitozicao do Vale do Naboa. Tomar, Escola Superior de Tecnologia de Tomar.

———, 1991: A Arqueueologia da Morte: consideracoes a proposito da interpretacao dos contextos sepulcrais na regiao de Tomar. Boletim Cultural da Camara Municipal de Tomar, vol., 15: 267-91.

———, 1992: O rio Nabao ha 4000 anos. O Povoado da Fonte Quente e o mais antigo povoamento no vale do Nabao. Boletim Cultural da Camara Municipal de Tomar, vol, 17: 27-42.

———, 1993: Amoreira: Novos elemontos para la compreensao da transicao do Mesolitico para o Neolitico no Alto Ribatejo,. Boletim Cultural da Camara Municipal de Tomar, vol. 19.

Cruz, A.R. L. Oosterbeek 1993: Artes Tradicionais: a ceramica. Contributo para uma metodolgia de analise tecnomorfologica. Boletim Cultural da Camara Municipal de Tomar, vol. 19

———, 1991: Carta Atqueologica de Tomar. Revista de Ciencias Historicas da Universidade Portucalense Infante D. Henrique, vol., VI: 77-89.

———, 1992: Habotat et territores dans la Prehistoire recente dans le Haut-Ribatejo (Portugal). Mediterraneo, vol. 1: 79-93.

———, 1993: Gruta dos Ossos (Tomar). Um ossuario do Neolitico final, Boletim Cultural da Camara Municipal de Tomar, vol. 18.

———, 1993: Nossa Senhora das lapas - excavation of Prehistoric cave burials in Central Portugal. Papers of the Institute of Archaeology, vol. 4: 49-62.

———, 1994: O Alto Ribatejo e o Mediterraneo Espaco continuo ou hierarquizado? Trabalhos de Antropologia e Etnologia, vol. 34.

———, 1994:.Echoes from the East: the western network. An insight to unequal and combined development, 7000-2000 BC. London, University of London, PhD, Dissertation (2 vols.)

———, 1995: Megalitismo e Necropolizacao no Alto Ribatejo - o III° mileno, Actas do Seminario "O Megalitismo no Centro de Portugal" 20 a 22 de Novembro/1992 Mangual de (no prelo)

7

Prehistory and History

Giancarlo Susini

Relationship between Prehistory and History

If history is regulated by time, it does not seem possible—or at least it is arguable—that there could be time outside history. We all know that, in our everyday life, time spent in waiting-rooms is usually difficult to measure, so much so that the moment in which the waiting ends is conditioned by the psychosis created by the waiting. When the mind turns to prehistory, a large part of public opinion suffers from (or nourishes) similar feelings to those felt by a patient in a waiting-room. Likewise prehistory is almost universally considered as the waiting-room of history.

With this basic thought in mind—and as a scholar used to living among ancient writings—approach the subject of the relationship between prehistory and history, wondering whether for both (academic subjects? or divisions of human time?) it may be possible to apply the criteria of a search for absolute, comparative or relative chronology and how it may be possible to use the notion of culture, or that of area, land or horizon or, lastly of *facies*. I also wonder if it is possible not to abandon the habit of searching for the *causae efficientes* among men and particularly in the different environments and for the *causae finales* (to use terms codified by the doctrine of historians) among the different societies, of all levels. Finally, I feel it is necessary to evaluate the relationship between prehistory and history as interpreted by current opinion, including that of the general public; let us not forget those opinions, and try to understand them.

To complete this approach, we can ask ourselves to what extent the interpretative categories of succession, process and duration are applicable and effective when dealing with prehistory —when it is anchored to time. In other words, whether prehistory can be interpreted using a historical method; and even whether it is permissible to look for prehistory and history in the "novelty" of every single moment or event, whether it is possible to ensure for both prehistory and history the temporal principles of continuity and renewal, whether we should be content to distinguish between prehistory and history on the basis that the former lacks the "account" of time perception, and therefore lacks too the meaning of before and after, of cause and effect, of synchrony and diachrony.

The doctrine produces many ideas which often lead one to assimilate prehistorical science to anthropology, to ethnography (do we finally give up trying to look in prehistory for the reasons for difference in skin colour, or for the roots of communication, and first of all of language, or finally for the acknowledgement, also from an ideological point of view, of the concept of original primates?) and to ecology one cannot deny that, throughout the long life of the earth and of men, many landscapes have been formed and modified, and one cannot abandon the search for reciprocal relationships between men and environment: it is epistemologically difficult to deny the legitimacy of paleo-ethnology or paleo-ecology, and this therefore presupposes specific research methods for an "ancient" part of time, defined or not as the waiting-room of history, as something "upon a time". A common place (attenuated when we speak of proto-history, in other words of a discipline in which the literature peeps out from far away observatories in the space of prehistory) gives to prehistory the essential help of archaeology, when, on the other hand, history feeds mainly on philology. Fortunately we are used to thinking about philology also by evaluating a monumental context or a collection of objects or an ancient inscription, in which we do not exclude the text, nor do we ignore the monumental and environmental context, or the effectiveness of graphic design.

Signs to Gather Evidences

In discerning the general meaning of the relationship between prehistory and history, a role is played by the events which, in every age, have lead to the knowledge, even superficial, of "different" cultures within other cultures able to codify the data of the former as is what happened among the civilizations of the so-called classical world with regard to the *peregrini* or "barbarians", or when they moved away from the lines or into the hot lands where *sunt leones*. Often by crossing stylistic features specific to prehistorical science with others is considered to belong to ethnography and anthropology, the events of exploration, subjection and colonization of countries defined as belonging to a "third" or "new" world have enriched and sometimes dissipated the concept of prehistory. The most recent studies of the formation of human settlements, as also of cities, codify, for example, the preference for coastal areas (ancient knowledge was often based on circumnavigation, for river mouths, for crossable fords, for defensible heights), for shaded areas around large deserts, and thus emphasizing the diversity—and therefore the hierarchy between different environments, both natural and human. Often, knowledge is reduced to picturesque stereotypes, which even encourage a comparison between societies belonging to an ancient prehistory and those more recent or contemporary which are not yet involved in industrial economy. In this context of impulsive and summary beliefs, the terms and concepts of cultures and civilizations are applied indiscriminately. The former are retrieved, in small pieces, by explorers or travellers in search of shelter in caves or of fossils, while the latter dominate, are even legitimized —and each of them in its own time plays its role in civilizing. This does not exclude but on the contrary, it confirms, the invaluable contribution of mythographers, navigators, cartographers and explorers, whether they tell of the existence of the Arimaspi, or are the first to reach the Galapagos. Inevitably, the scenary, situations and parabolas of prehistory—as current opinion and even doctrine see it—are measured and known according to the descriptions of the professional (or occasional) historiographers who have picked up the traces. It is then the role of doctrine to decodify the fabulous narrations and the retrospective sequences which ancient historiography (often mixed with mythography) has handed down.

The traces, or vestiges—as some scholars define them—are a useful platform from which to spy on the relationship between prehistory and history, if we realize that knowledge, however acquired, uses "signs" (traces, vestiges) which are the result of electric processes of selection and of heuristic and retrieval operations. This is an initial consideration regarding the method: archaeological maps have had the merit of linking traces of landscapes and environments, and also to the physical and human context of the moment in which they were drawn up. Finally, there is no knowledge without an appreciation of the processes of data transmission and tradition, in the same way that the history of prehistorical discoveries is not distinguished from past or present historiography. Prehistory too is represented in the historians' Wunderkammer. Pliny the Elder's *Naturalis Historia* aligns phenomena and episodes of the most ancient life, still being told and referred to in the literature of his time.

Transition

Within contemporary imagination, a state of being "prehistorical" involves conditions or real technological backwardness and of cultural isolation, found in situations and events throughout time as according to a famous expression, prehistory is the only condition in which the poor have a place in history. For many, "prehistorical" is a term which defines remote situations, irrecoverable and scarcely imaginable: it is not clear whether prehistorical should be swapped with "ancient"—and therefore with something venerable—or with "old", and therefore definitely condemned to the past and the useless.

Finally, a current metaphor considers prehistorical the phase of formation of any technical and cultural phenomenon, if fire enables man to transform matter, Prometheus's myth represents its incunabulum. In an epistemological context, the mere fact that prehistorical science dedicates so much attention to physical and environmental investigation supports the semantic temptation to confuse prehistorical with primeval. In the common mind, folklore helps the living retrieval of traces of past behaviour.

To a scholar of (ancient) history, the zeal of the scholars of prehistory seems to be primarily aimed at codifying certain basic (anthropological, one could say) aspects of human presence, which are, men's needs and fulfilment of them.

The passage from one place to the next, the use of hand and arm, the relationship with the land and its resources (primarily water), the culture of fire, movement (on foot, on animals—and therefore man's relationship with them), perception of sources of energy other than human strength, such as wind, rain, water current (and therefore movement on wood and orientation with boom and rudder), animal draught, handwork, and therefore tools, made of wood, stone, bone (teeth, shells), metal (with associated techniques), also the use of ochre, the treatment of skins and fibres, the evolved use of instruments (produced and moved by the hand or arm) for cutting and hitting; hunting, capture, harvesting, handling of grains, of powders, of resins, human communication, which cannot be recuperated in speech, though at the most through dispositions on the ground or in glyphs, which are more eloquent; appropriation of the environment, along paths and tracks, waterways or on ridges, with settlements in caves or in huts, sometimes sheltered by bushes or woods near water sources (*lucus*), by mastering and harnessing the horse; habits in other words a *traditio* which enables the discovery of events, and therefore the description of processes, retrieved, on occasion, from myths.

In the network of such seriation of research, the historian glimpses a number of "turning-points", in which it seems to him that men are the protagonists of new orders which he can codify in the following way: settlement on the land, in a permanent fashion and as an alternative to nomadic movement, and therefore with house furnishings and with an organized structure: within defined perimeters, sometimes of a geometrical shape, getting to know and putting into practice alignment and crossing, learning to read the stars, and taking careful notice of sunlight and weather; the evolved use of numbers, of metric marks (notches on sticks or stones), the awareness of time rhythm (day, cycles of the moon, seasons), complex geometry applied to the organization on the land, the network structure in the lattice-work of the hut and in mats or fabrics (looms); evolved treatment of hand-made articles (wooden, stone, bone, metallic or clay) as tools, treatment of stone surfaces (scrapers, spatulas), cut and lamination of stone; the practice of graffito and engraving; treatment of wool (combs); technique of spinning, minerary and metallurgical techniques and practices; evolved culture of fire; reference to the sky from a cultural point of view; the role of megaliths and peaks or points, messages drawn on the ground, and any glyph on walls or rocks; the sense of collective, or already historical, memory offered to a celestial dialogue, and therefore to a heavenly recipient (a indecipherable as the anonymous public casting an eye today over graffiti art); the representation of the face in a circle (clypeiform), reproduced as a mask, with complex semantics; the culture of symbolic and figurative reproduction (head-shaped vases); drawing of the hand, formation of symbols, ritual practices, cult of the dead, memory of ancestors, also as a precognition of temporal processes, aggregation of clans, profile of the economy, resources, production (cattle breeding, farming), accumulation, processing and exchange of products, class relations, hierarchies, appropriation of resources and of land, protection of the environment in settlements; offence and defence, hand weapons and throwing weapons; clothing, the culture of the body; figurative language on objects, monuments and glyphs; decoration; walking, migrating (move or transhumance or work or seasonal alternations, or new appropriations; even Theodoric's tent can become a mausoleum); once again the horse; the wheel; the evolved knowledge of energy.

Archeometry as a Tool

Euristics and knowledge in prehistory are often piloted by exact or physical sciences, useful both for the retrieval of micro-environments, and for the appreciation of cultural horizons and of their respective evolutions. The use of such sciences for dating cannot be substituted. Geological and biological data, paleo-ecological considerations, assessment of climates, are all part of the entrance hall (let us forget the word waiting-room) of a *domus* where the *tablinum* corresponds to the workshop, or rather to the modern man's place of work. With such methods, fed on all anthropological doctrines, prehistorical science teaches history the practice of the entrance hall, it possesses the threshold where history opens up. The experience of an epigrapher would lead us to consider methods and results of the prehistorical science as a "contrarindex" to understand suffixes and desinences, i.e. the real words of an ancient text: in this sense, archeometry renders meaningful much of the data useful to the historian.

Usefulness of Historiography

A question, which comes up is that if prehistorical science is an irreplaceable viaticum for the work of the historian, does this lead us to imagine—land by land, horizon by horizon, age by age—a useful criterion to decipher the transition from prehistory (from its time, since it has a place in time, aligning its methods with those of historical sciences) to history? To a scholar of ancient writings as also other scholars, it seems natural to set this transition as a chapter of the history of human communication, more specifically towards an aware and transmissible knowledge, in stable and lasting forms, of the temporal sequences of a given society. Though this is nothing new, in fact, if anything, the confirmation of the anchoring to a historiographic event, which imposes both an evolution of the minds and of languages and the lasting instruments of communication, i.e. writing in its broadest sense—historiographies, or in any case the security of documented tradition. A stage of culturalization, one could say, on condition that one bear in mind that often culturalization disguises the manipulation of past cultures by dominant cultures, a culturalization which is often manifested in the form of literacy, the myth of Cadmus can be significant in this context, even if the historiography which descends from the literacy therein recounted cannot be classified as primitive, compared with eulogies and catalogues produced by the Near and Middle East. Undoubtedly, a "historical" communication presupposes the conscious identification of a particular society with a given culture for, through this, it becomes easier to define the respective meanings of the two terms—culture and civilization—often used in a transgressive way.

We have already said how, traditionally, the history of a culture (of a people, a society, and so of a civilization) is considered relevant to protohistory when it is a different historiography that speaks about it. It should be noted that in this case it is possible to pinpoint, almost anywhere and at any time, the knowledge of groups and social classes who are not masters of a direct historiography. Political and cultural "periferies"—a definition some dislike—are manifested as such precisely because of their social position. In such cases, of even greater significance are the collections of objects and the monumental context, often solitary witnesses of extinct or feeble histories, especially the relationship between archaeology and historiography leads to results of great critical interest.

Nevertheless, knowledge through communication with glyphs and writings cannot be considered as a categorical temporal diaphragm. By reviewing some of the "turning-points" mentioned above as revealing new cultural, economic and social assets, we can observe the almost historiographic significance of certain phenomena, useful to reveal the historical even incomplete grammar of certain civilizations. We are referring to those marks on the ground which reveal advanced calculation methods, advanced geometries, complex hierarchical roles and complementarity of social classes, techniques of treasuring and of market which are recognizable even without the assistance of documentary archives. To this should be added complex symbolic languages and cultural apparatuses strongly linked with collective identities. As for rightfully called—at least in the doctrinal tradition —"historical" cultures, the notions which result from such assets are correctly put side by side with geological data, results of biological analyses, ecological sceneries, and stratigraphies, when these are interpreted as part of the documentation of processes as in a vision corresponding to the reciprocal relationships between men and environments.

Combination of Prehistory and History to Delve into the Past

At times, it is suggested that the patient, wonderful work of scientists of prehistory should be really appreciated as the core of the work of the historian, another lantern to illuminate the future. This work deals with the virtual reconstruction of the past, and to this end there is a coalescence between the humble knowledge of the history of everyday life, and the results of the exegetic syndromes practiced by the scholars of prehistory. I believe it is reasonable to ask if such experiences can be useful for the virtual prefiguration of the future, helping us to perceive the dynamics which project the human parabola from the present into the future.

Prehistory and history are two subjects for a great science which can throw light on the future, on transformations and destructions of landscapes, on the monstrous numerical relationship between man and the planet, on the menaces which predict so many more old people and so much more hunger, and the permanent alteration of new continents in the management of resources and human order.

8

Art and Conceptuality of the *Homo Sapiens*

Emmanuel Anati

The first intellectual expressions of humankind lead us back to time immemorial. The discovery of our roots raises profound questions that affect the very identity of our species.

In some prehistoric sites it has been noticed that hominids used to collect, transport and store stones and animal bones of particular shapes or colours, already during the Lower Palaeolithic period. It is not easy to decide whether this attitude towards collecting should be regarded as an indication of certain intellectual capacities. In order to do this, it would be useful to understand the aims and the purposes of such behaviours.

What is the meaning, in terms of conceptuality, of the symmetry which Acheulian hunters gave to their amygdales 5,00,000 years ago? These are sharp instruments worked on two sides, on which a sinuous blade forms along the perimeter where the two faces meet. According to our twentieth century taste, these tools are very elegant from an aesthetic point of view. It has not yet been ascertained whether this shape, which is considered slender and elegant today, was motivated by practical reasons or by more aesthetic demands. Some scholars have explained the shape of the amygdale with the intellectual capacity of its creators; of course these capacities would be even greater if apart from its practical purposes, the symmetry of this tool were motivated by aesthetic needs. This idea is not implausible, but still needs to be verified.

The signs engraved on stones and bones coming from European sites, have been dated back to very ancient times, especially by some scholars including Francois Bordes (1969), Piero Leonardi (1975) and, more recently, R.G. Bednarik (1995). Some fragments from the Lower Palaeolithic period engraved with scratches and signs are known which if they were found to be intentional and justified by cognitive factors, would be an indication of attempts, not necessarily graphic or aesthetic in nature, but at the execution of signs possibly of a numeric kind, indicating the presence of symbolism and conceptuality. Some groups of lines engraved on stones and bones, from Bilzingsleben in Germany, suggest a sort of "game" inspired by the discovery that with a spike it was possible to draw signs (D. Mania & U. Mania, *Deliberate Engravings on Bone Artefacts of Homo Erectus*, 1988). There have also been reports about an alleged Acheulian "female statue" in Israel, but this is probably a *ludum naturae*, a trick of nature (see also N. Goren-Inbar, 1986). There have also been reports about Acheulian stone art in India dating back to more than 3,00,000 years and other similar questionable findings.

Occasional findings have been made with signs of rubbing or usage, covered with lines and other non-figurative engravings or in some cases scratches and parallel lines both in Europe and in the Near East which date back to the period of Musterian culture, also described as Middle Palaeolithic in technical literature. The dating and arguments about these findings, however, do not always allow for their precise collocation. For the moment the only substantial engraving attributed to the Middle Palaeolithic is a group of cupels on a piece of stone found in La Ferrassie, in the Dordogne region, whose dating is also uncertain.

Neanderthal men have left in their habitation sites, rare bone fragments with engravings, parts of which reveal traces of working or attempts at cutting by using a chert, while others are graphically intentional, such as a zigzag engravings found in Bacho-Kiro in Bulgaria. Some of these probably have a numeric meaning. On the cover stone of the tomb in La Ferrassie, some cupels are engraved, cup-shaped holes which have been interpreted in different ways by the scholars; some say they serve a practical purpose, for others they are an early figurative attempt whose representative meaning has been explained in various ways.

In Quneitra on the Golan Heights in the Syrian–Palestine area, a chert fragment has been discovered on the surface of which parallel lines and concentric semicircles are drawn on a layer of Musterian culture, dated at about 54,000 years ago by using the ESR (Electron Spin Resonance) method (A. Marshack, *A Middle Paleolithic Symbolic Composition from the Golan-Heights*, 1996).

Fragments of colouring materials, such as okra red or manganese oxide, have often been found in Musterian layers, some of them show traces of use, sharpening on the point, signs of rubbing. They were definitely used to colour something, probably human bodies or the skins and fibres which men used to make clothing and other tools. Unfortunately the organic substances have not been preserved and so we can only make hypotheses about them. What is certain is that these products served to colour something which is a clear sign of an aesthetic or symbolic research, that is an intellectual fact in itself.

It is therefore possible to say that Neanderthal men have left some bone fragments with engraved markings. It is also possible to talk about the use of colourings, but there are no sufficient indications of a visual language and thus of a visual art.

In Africa, especially in Tanzania and Namibia, colouring materials that seem to have been used were found in archaeological layers inside caves with stone art on many layers covering the last 50,000 years. Once again it is not possible to say what exactly was being coloured and when humans started to produce art.

Neanderthal men lived in Europe and the Near East between 1,00,000 and 35,000 years ago and produced stone objects on fragments of a Musterian kind; during the same period in East Africa and the Near East there were men already very similar from a physical point of view to the *Homo Sapiens* that arrived in Europe at the beginning of the Upper Palaeolithic period. More than 50,000 years ago, in Tanzania, they had stone products including highly specialized and diversified "blade" tools: blades, spikes, stylets, scratchers and microliths of the kind used in Europe and the Near East about 35,000 years ago at the beginning, that is, of the Upper Palaeolithic period.

Neanderthal men have been classified by some scholars as *Homo sapiens neanderthalensis*. We refer to them as Neanderthal men, using the term *sapiens* only for the individuals who arrived in Europe during the Upper Palaeolithic period; we have also dropped the redundant second *sapiens* from the term *Homo sapiens sapiens.*

The expression *Homo sapiens* is used by scholars in many different ways. For some, it only refers to individuals whose skeleton has some modern somatic characteristics. The latter have been found in some individuals for more than 1,00,000 years, while other archaic skeletal traits can still be found, although very rarely, in some individuals. For other scholars, the expression *sapiens* refers to the brain characteristics of the individual and, in particular, the ability to synthesize, abstract and associate ideas revealed by the production of visual art and by the production of complex, highly specialized product groups with precisely diversified forms. These signs of "knowledge" can be found in Europe, the Near East and in the Mediterranean area during the Upper Palaeolithic period.

Visual art, with its representative figures or pictograms and signs or ideograms, voluntarily combined in groups, is a phenomenon that as far as we know originated about 40,000 years ago. Graphical ability involves the presence of analithic capacities, association and abstraction which already seem to appear in Neanderthal men while the question of what happened previously is still open. Although various attempts and reports have been made on the subject according to the author, for the moment there are no findings which can be defined as art dating back to the Middle or Lower Palaeolithic periods.

With the arrival of the *Homo sapiens* and his ability to produce art forms, the presence of some traits that today are considered essentially, "human" is revealed. These beings actually appear to have acquired most of the characteristics we regard as "human" and also had many of the communication and planning skills which have been known since then up to the present day.

The First Signs Evident

Some general remarks can be made about the ability to conceptualize. Creativity and imagination lead both to rationality and to irrational expressions. The discovery of the self and the relation between the subject and the surrounding world has always encouraged the search for "supernatural" factors which have definitely played an essential role during the formation period of human beings. Every experience, every new situation, every unsolved problem might have been attributed to sacred reasons.

Apart from the finding of tombs that show indications of funeral ceremonies and are an essential source of information about ideology, there are other aspects which could be interpreted as forms of conceptualization. Numerous archaeological discoveries have been explained with religious motivations, but there is scarce evidence to justify this idea. At the moment there are a number of data that have been interpreted in a religious way but in most cases there are no decisive or sufficiently plausible factors.

As the author already wrote (E. Anati *Le Radici della Cultura*, 1992: *La Religione Originale* 1995) several findings seem to demonstrate specifically ritual attitudes that have been defined as the cult of bones, of aggressive animals such as the bear and the wolf, the cult of objects, rites of passage and propitiatory rites. The few certain findings have led to a massive production of related literature because they have stimulated the reasoning and the imagination of scholars.

The most ancient certain document showing a belief of humans in the supernatural is connected with one of the phenomena that has not ceased to stimulate human thinking ever since, concerning a reality that affects us all, namely the end of life and the facing of death. This is also linked with the need that humans have to explain to themselves not only what death is and what comes after it, but also the significance of life. This is a very profound question which humans have always wondered about and has led to suggestions, created religions, philosophies and scientific disciplines, and which still has not found a satisfactory answer.

The ritual attitude towards the dead does not seem to derive directly from a rational logic based on the three basic instincts of eating, defending one's life and continuing the species though, on an irrational level it is connected with these three factors. The dead were buried in sepulchral areas with a constant ritual common to various places in the European and Asiatic area of the Musterian culture. This shows that there was a uniform widespread tradition. In the Near East, in the cave of Skhul on Mount Carmel, in Central Asia in Teshik-Tash in Europe at Le Moustier and La Chapelle-aux-Saints in France there are clear analogies in the way the living treated their dead.

During the Middle Palaeolithic period there are already signs of "grave goods". At Le Moustier, in a grave that raises many questions, the author of the discovery, Denis Peyrony, has found animal bones still in an articulate position, although they had been cut on both sides. The scholar was thus able to say that a piece of meat had been placed near the dead.

La Ferrassie is probably the most interesting burial area of the Middle Palaeolithic period in Europe. It contains several tombs and here again food has been placed near the dead. The animal bones are what remains of the meat offered.

Neanderthal men show a strange behaviour that is, the act of burying, meant acknowledging that the person is no longer alive, that his/her life has come to an end. However, they put food near him so he could find something to eat. Does this mean the person was not completely "dead"? Should the food provided and buried near the dead persons have been the meal they would take before reaching the final destination? This simple act might be an indication of a belief in life after death. The hope of an afterlife has not ceased motivating the behaviour of human beings ever since. In any case, the ritual attitude towards the dead indicates the belief that the latter still had vital energies and thus deserved care and consideration. If there still was some energy present in them, it could be used for good or evil. Certainly these emotional factors led the living to take care of their dead.

During the Upper Palaeolithic period art reveals a similar attitude towards animals. Dreams and other unconscious phenomena might have led to the ideology at the basis of conceptuality.

Middle Palaeolithic men living in Eurasia had a precise conception of life after death, which probably involved the belief in a passage or a journey from this life to the next. This also seems to imply the belief in a supernatural, or better extraterrestrial world. In other words, we can say that these beings believed in the survival of the "soul" once the body was dead. The dead shifted from one world to another, carrying with them the remembrance of the good or bad relations they had with the living who, in turn, would reach the same destination one day.

These speculations on irrationality develop together with the indications of the presence of "rational" thinking. Apart from the artistic forms, the behaviour towards the dead and the presence of objects which probably had a ritual use, such complexity of human thinking is revealed by the appearance of a new technology for the production of stone tools for daily use which become much more complex and articulate, thus implying a rational use of the raw material and a planned production of the artefacts.

There are also other data supporting the presence of an articulate conceptuality before the arrival of the *Homo sapiens* (E. Anati, *La Religione Originale*, 1995). It is certainly possible to talk about precedents and the presence of an articulate conceptuality already before the appearance of the *Homo sapiens* during the Middle Palaeolithic period. There is evidence that men practised ritual cannibalism, the cult of skulls and of animals. The available data can be interpreted in various ways and, even though there are clear signs of ritualistic behaviour, it is not always clear to what extent this can be defined as a religious attitude. However, it is definitely possible to talk about conceptuality at least since the beginning of the Middle Palaeolithic period, that is for the past 1,00,000 years. In particular, with reference to the attitude towards the dead, there are concepts concerning the vision of an extra-terrestrial life, the belief in life after death and intellectual considerations about human existence.

In the Syrian-Palestine area, during the transitional phase between the Middle and Upper Palaeolithic period, the oldest sanctuary has been discovered where humans show a particular interest in interpreting nature and where this interest becomes a sort of "proto-art" whose protagonists are probably *sapiens* in their own right.

The data concerning the intellectual aspects before the arrival of *Homo sapiens* mostly come from the area where the largest amount of research has been carried out, namely Europe and the

Syrian-Palestine area. Much less is known about the other two continents where traces of previous hominids have been found. Africa and Asia are virtually unknown from this point of view and will undoubtedly be a source of many surprises in the future. In America and Oceania, in spite of statements to the contrary and occasional announcements of "revolutionary" discoveries, there are no certain elements showing the presence of man before the widespread expansion of the *Homo sapiens*. This is not impossible, but it has not been proved yet, even though some scholars will not agree with the author.

The clearest documents concerning conceptuality, for the moment, come from Europe and the Near East and refer to the cult of the dead. They reveal human concern with mortality and the search for an afterlife. It is not yet possible to talk about these phenomena in terms of a well-structured religion, but there were definitely beliefs, concepts and even rules to be followed, traditional rites concerning the way of burying the dead and the choice of the place. Those who did this were certainly representatives of the Neanderthal group, which became completely and mysteriously extinct with the arrival of the *Homo sapiens*.

The above-mentioned sanctuary, known as site HK86B of Har Karkom in the Israeli desert of Negev, shows the first signs of the conceptual factors which will be found later in Palaeolithic wall art.

The first signs of structuring of the religious concept, with precise rules, are shown by the phenomenon of artistic creativity in humans living during the Upper Palaeolithic period. Inside the sanctuary-caves, more than 3,00,000 years ago, the *Homo sapiens* created objects for ritual use, produced wonderful works of art inspired by mythology and by other aspects of conceptuality and held rites linked to his beliefs. The wall and furniture art, the findings made inside these "sanctuaries" bear witness to the existence and development of extremely complex beliefs, if compared to the Middle Palaeolithic period, they also testify to the presence of widespread ritual practices and of places set aside for intellectual activities such as artistic creativity and worship.

Conceptuality of the *Homo sapiens*

The Darwinian theory according to which art and conceptuality gradually developed from the Pithecanthropus onwards, is being questioned in the light of recent research discoveries. Today the conceptual and technological evolution are seen as a series of steps; each of them being the result of a combination of causes, but especially of new mental capacities.

The human species have been inhabiting the earth for more than four million years. During its existence man's capacity to express himself and operate in various ways have developed. Sometimes the production of a new tool is the cause and effect of new mental skills, sometimes changes in the climate and in the resources have forced behavioural adaptations. With the arrival of *Homo sapiens* a revolution took place in the mechanism of logic, in the way of thinking and in the abstraction and synthesis capacities; this is an unprecedented revolution as far as we know, both in the stages of human evolution as well as of other animal species.

Although Darwinian theories are still alive in some environments and attempts have been made at attributing visual art findings at a very ancient date, comparative analysis provides increasing evidence that there is a connection between the arrival of *Homo sapiens* and the origin of the art.

A series of data, which will be examined later on, seems to point to a solution of the debate among evolutionists following various trends on the subject of the origin of the species. The Darwinian theory according to which *Homo sapiens* would be the result of an evolution process with parallel manifestations in various parts of the globe, appears to be in contrast with some common features of "sapiens" humanity, which would explain it as the result of a series of coincidences unlikely to happen again. These same coincidences, which will be discussed later, seem to indicate that these new human beings had a common origin, that is they originated in a well-defined area, possibly as a result of a particular configuration or of some other possible factors leading to precise microgenetic mutations. Starting from their birthplace, presumably in Africa, they began to reproduce and to reach the other continents. Recent findings also seem to indicate that while the Neanderthal men lived in Europe and the Near East, individuals very similar to the *Homo sapiens* as for mental capacities and methods used for the creation and use of tools, who arrived in Europe during the Upper Palaeolithic period, were already developing in Eastern and austral Africa.

The hypothesis of a union between a primitive "father" and "mother" that originated our species, brings us back to the collective mythical memory of the Adam and Eve epic, wonderful allegory of the original myth. Two individuals, or rather two groups of individuals, would be the forefathers of the *Homo sapiens*, a new kind of human being with a data-storing capacity much higher than his predecessors, with a longer childhood period and a particular set of somatic trait, but especially with very peculiar brain capacities which provided him with a new emotional dimension and intellectual disposition. These are all mechanisms of association, symbolization, abstraction and sublimation that are still part of the universal characteristics of the *Homo sapiens*.

Humans also became artists, and may be art production is not only a capacity, but rather a natural need for human beings. From that moment on, humans acquired a certain visual, conceptual and communicative outlook, which fits into the framework of a new way of reacting to the surrounding world and relating to it. Without these qualities, the human relations that characterize us would not exist, we would not have deep emotional and affective relations, the kind of interaction that allows us to communicate and exchange ideas with other humans approaching them with intensity and awareness would not exist, and our mind would not ask itself the questions without which no intellectual thinking goes on.

When prehistoric art in the various continents was studied and regarded as a series of local isolated phenomena, the world record was easily attributed to every oldest local manifestation discovered. Europeans thought art had originated on their continent at the beginning of the Upper Palaeolithic period, their Indian colleagues maintained that art had originated in India more or less during the same period and the same can be said about Russian scholars who had found the primary, and according to some the oldest, nucleus of artistic expression around Lake Baikal in Siberia. Furthermore, the discoveries made by W.E. Wendt in

Namibia had provided reliable very ancient dating, so that some scholars at the beginning of the 70s suggested that art might have originated in Africa, thus raising a heated debate. Now Australians claim they have the record of the most ancient findings.

In Namibia the digging carried out by W.E. Wendt inside the Apollo 11 cave brought to light various stone tablets with pictures of animals, some of which polychromatic, on an archaeological level dated by three Carbon 14 examinations respectively at 28,400, 26,700 and 26,300 years (W.E. Wendt, 1976). Dendrochronology shows that C 14 dates tend to make findings younger and have therefore to be adjusted; in fact they should be increased by 15 to 20 per cent in order to calculate the real age. The fact remains that they are polychromatic, refined and highly developed works which certainly show the existence of a long-standing tradition before them. It is surprising to note the stylistic and thematic similarity between these paintings and other artistic products found in Europe and in other continents. In Europe, however, polychromatic figures of the same kind are Magdalenian and date back to about 10,000-15,000 years later. For the moment the most ancient elements have not been identified, but cave paintings, in the same style as the tablets found by Wendt have been discovered on the walls of small caves laid in stratigraphy above older figures.

In Tanzania a series of very ancient cave paintings has been found, one of their most recent phases corresponding, from a stylistic point of view, to the tablets of Apollo 11. The beginning date of the Tanzanian sequence is not known; at the foot of a painted wall in a small cave, however, residues of colouring substances have been found which show signs of use, in archaeological layers dated with the C14 method at more than 40,000 years ago (E. Anati, *BCSP*, vol. 23, 1986, p. 15). Austral Africa certainly has many more surprises in store. Systematic research carried out on the stratigraphic sequences of cave paintings which have been known for a very long time, would alone provide a great contribution to our knowledge of the evolution phases in the longest sequences of cave art known to date.

In North Africa, the most ancient works of art currently dated are in Acacus, Libya, and date back to the end of Pleistocene, about 12,000 years ago according to Fabrizio Mori (F. Mori.,

Valcamonica Symposium '68, 1970, p. 345). They represent the typical cave art of archaic hunters, in a style widespread also in the Sahara, in the Tassili-n-Agger in Algeria and in the Tchadian Ennedi.

In Europe the first graphic signs, dated at about 34,000 years ago, were probably made at the beginning of the Upper Palaeolithic period, which means they are signs of the oldest presence of the *Homo sapiens* on the continent. But the wonderful and universally known polychromatic paintings found in the Laseaux and Altamira caves date back to the Magdalenian period which started 16,000 years ago.

In the case of Asia, the oldest works of furniture art known to date are some female statues found on the shores of Lake Baikal in Siberia dating back to about 34,000 years ago (non-adjusted C14 dating) (Abramova, *BCSP*, vols. 25-26, 1990, p. 81). In India a layer with fragments of decorated ostrich eggs has been found in a small decorated cave dating back to about 25,000 years ago (C 14) (E Anati, *BCSP*, vol. 221, 1984, p. 13). The report that some cave engravings had been found under archaeological layers more than 2,00,000 years old is not reliable.

In the Near East, the most ancient works known are probably cave engravings with fine traits "in Central Arabia" representing ideograms, animals and anthropomorphic figures, in particular female, which have been found near the Dahatami wells and in sites nearby. The stratigraphy shows three engraving phases by archaic hunters, which probably bear witness to a long iconographic tradition during late Pleistocene up until the beginning of Holocene. For the moment, no precise datings are known (E. Anati, *Rock Art of Central Arabia*, vols. 3, 4, 1972, 1974).

In Australia, recent research date some cave engravings at more than 40,000 years ago. The methods used are actually questionable and further tests are necessary before accepting this information. The data acquired concern later datings. In the Koonalda cave, near Adelaide and on other sites, the oldest cave engravings date back to about 22,000 C 14 years ago (R.G. Bednarik, *BCSP*, vol. 22, 1985, p. 83), but these are apparently non-figurative signs. The oldest confirmed dates for figurative works in Australia come from Laura in the York peninsula. These have been found in a cave covered with archaeological layers, from which C 14 dates of about 17,000 years have been obtained: they are mainly vulva signs and other ideograms of the same kind as those found in France during the Aurignatian and Perigordian eras.

In America for the moment the most reliable ancient date we know is about 17,000 years (C 14) in the State of Piaui in Brazil which refers to the archaeological layer of an engraved cave in which fragments of wall defoliation with painting residues have been found (N. Guidon, *L. Anthropologie*, vol. 87/2, 1983, p. 257). In the same area, remains of pieces of okra chalk with signs of use have been found in even more ancient layers. It is likely that there are even older works to be found both in North America and in the South: however recent reports about findings dating back to a much older age should be subject to further analysis.

There has been much speculation about the origin of various sources of artistic production. As research continues and more discoveries are made, we shall probably have to resort to the theory of a single origin. The certain dates currently available seem to indicate a process of art diffusion, but we still do not know how this happened; the theory of a connection between the diffusion of art and of *Homo sapiens*, however, seems to be gaining ground.

Previous episodes in the evolution of *Homo sapiens* have shown that Eastern and austral Africa has played the role of a large genetic laboratory where nature carried out its experiments for this is where a large amount of fossil remains have been found indicating the physical evolution of the species and this is probably where the *Sapiens* formed, that direct ancestor of ours responsible among other things for artistic creativity.

Concerning the origins of *Homo sapiens*, the findings scattered in various continents seem to indicate that these beings quickly developed from their place of origin in Africa and conquered the world in a few thousand years.

Part of the heritage of the *Homo sapiens* is the capacity and the need of expression through a visual language. Maybe there are also analogies between the human need to explore the territory and to explore inside the self, of asking questions and also suggesting answers on the subject of life and existence. Apart from the physical development, there is also a diffusion of this new human skill. This distribution appears strangely homogeneous throughout the earth, so much so that it is possible to say that, wherever *Homo sapiens* arrived, there are traces of artistic creativity.

The latest research shows that the various artistic expressions of the most ancient periods throughout the world are very similar in nature, because the same topic is chosen and the kinds of associations and ideas used undergo limited variations. It therefore seems relevant to talk about a single visual language, a single logic, a universal symbolism and structure of idea association all of which make up the mental image of the *Homo sapiens* whose footprints have been left on the rocky surfaces of all the continents.

Kinds of Art

A comparative analysis of prehistoric art on a global scale has revealed surprising similarities between what is known about the five continents. On the basis of the reflected economy, four categories of prehistoric art have been identified which refer respectively to: (1) archaic hunters; (2) developed hunters; (3) shepherds and breeders and (4) mixed economy populations. Within these categories prehistoric art, on a global level, shows four kinds of pictograms: (1) anthropomorphic; (2) zoomorphic; (3) topographic and roof-shaped; (4) objects. Apart from the pictograms there are also ideograms and psychograms. The latter are mostly present in the art forms of archaic hunters and too few of them are known as yet to be able to define categories. Ideograms are in turn divided into three groups: (a) anatomic; (b) numerical; (c) conceptual. These groupings cover virtually all the graphemes that have been found both in caves and in furniture art throughout the world.

Prehistoric art shows that the main concerns were about specific questions with an existential and philosophical character, aimed at finding the answer to difficult questions which humans asked themselves concerning their identity and the manifestations of the world around them. The basic relation was that with the animal world from which they drew their means of living.

Landscapes are very rare, as are also paintings of plants and personalized portraits. As far as we know landscapes are virtually absent among the populations of archaic hunters and developed hunters. Among breeders' populations anthropic landscapes can be found almost always without plants and without a horizon: if the term landscapes can be used they are usually paintings with groups of huts and scenes of daily life or worship as they appear in the pastoral phases in various places in the Sahara or in central India. The cave engravings of the pastoral age in the Negev and in the Sinai show outlines of figures, cattle enclosures and large traps for gazelle hunting: there are pictures of cattle enclosures in the cave engravings made by bovine breeders on Mount Bego, in the French Maritime Alps.

Landscapes with a topographic definition are produced by small groups with complex economies. There is a fresco with the "plan" of the village and the mountain nearby in the Neolithic site of Catal Huyuk in Anatolia and there are plans of villages, habitations and fields in the cave art of the populations with complex economies of the Valcamonica.

As for the painting of plants, trees, flowers, fruits and leaves they are almost totally absent from the majority of prehistoric art because when these subjects are represented they are indicated by specific characteristics. For example in Tanzania, a sequence which lasted thousands of years has been found: all the plant paintings we know are concentrated in one single phase dating back to the end of Pleistocene or the beginning of Holocene between 12,000 and 8,000 years ago. The available data suggest that it is represented from the perspective of gatherers, not of hunters, even though it was painted during the period defined as that of "Archaic Hunters". This population was mainly vegetarian and made large use of drugs (*BCSP*, vol. 23).These exceptions, rare as they may be, exist and they are extremely interesting and relevant.

In each of the four categories mentioned there are elements called paradigms. This means recurring models, significant elements that appear throughout the whole category and all over the world. There are also preferences concerning the surface to be decorated—caves, shelters, open air-rocky surfaces. Inside the cave itself, or outside it, there can be a preference for horizontal, sloping, vertical or towards ceiling or roof.

In each category a definite choice seems to have been made about the surface onto which the paintings or engravings should be made and this is so repetitive that in all four cases it is possible to identify the favourite choices of shape and colour of the surfaces. A preliminary analysis shows that a very high percentage up to 85 per cent of all the paintings and engravings, meets these criteria. But there are always exceptions to the rule and the exceptions require an explanation. It appears in any case that there is a conceptual link between the work of art and the support chosen for it.

In many cases definite choices seem to have been made concerning the execution technique, both for painting and for engraving as well as in hack-hammer graffiti and in the various smoothing methods. There are recurring elements, but in our view they do not seem to reflect factors of acculturation or of diffusion. In some cases the kind of execution seems simply to be the result of a certain technological level or of a certain way of thinking; one could suppose that, even if the various populations did not communicate the respective techniques to one another, they reached similar conclusions no matter how far away and distant the places they lived in might be. This parallelism in their development cannot always have been brought about by external factors. Even long after the primary expansion of the *Homo sapiens* there are probably common matrices which produced similar "resonance" even thousands of years later. The study of these paradigms is fascinating because it brings us back to universal characteristics of our unconscious memory.

The themes, then, are extremely limited and repetitive. Among the archaic hunters and the developed hunters, in Europe, Asia, Africa, America and Australia the same range of figures can be found. The relative proportions of the four kinds of pictogram vary, but on the whole the associations seem to follow much the same associative syntax.

In the mentality of these populations there are aspects of the environment, economy and social life that simply seem to be beyond the concerns and interests expressed by their figurative range. The artists, be they hunters or members of other groups, made definite choices about the subject they represented. In the groups belonging to a mixed economy society, regional or local topics are found more frequently because they allow to define geographically limited characteristics.

Apart from the choice of the surface, the execution techniques, the themes and typology, size also plays an essential role in order to identify recurring characteristics.

In some places there is a preference for certain dimensions. For example, the large paintings of animals in real-life size or taller than 1.5 or 2 metres can be found almost exclusively in hunters' tribes and only in some groups of shepherds always in areas which are deserts today, especially in Arabia and in the Sahara area. In the cave art of peoples with mixed economies these images are very rare and in some areas they are totally absent. On the other hand, there are phases in the development of archaic hunters and developed hunters when small animal figures and even miniatures are found.

Another strange phenomenon has been observed in this respect that in the groups where animal figures are large, representations of humans are virtually absent, while in those populations where animal figures are smaller, the percentage of anthropomorphic figures is remarkably higher. This recurring phenomenon has not been explained yet.

In every group there are favourite and secondary subjects which means there is a sort of primary choice which is essential, inside which a further choice has been made. Alongside the dominant topics there are minor subjects and there are also repetitive elements, ideograms or other graphemes which always accompany the dominant representations. It is probably an oversimplification to say, as many have done, that in European Palaeolithic art, animal figures are dominant and by the same token the statement that animals are the dominant figures in archaic hunters' tribes throughout the world means approximating the question. Contrary to common opinion, though, there are few isolated animal figures and they are almost always accompanied by ideograms in larger amount than the animal images and by other associated pictograms. The latter are often bigger than the ideograms. The isolated animal was not enough to represent what humans wished to express and it often appears as the main "word", the subject of sentences consisting of pictograms and ideograms.

In all the groups of works by archaic hunters known today, there are constant ways of associating pictograms and ideograms, that is figurative themes and repetitive graphemes where the sign cannot be immediately translated into an image. It is therefore clear enough that the understanding of the messages they contain depends on the comprehension of the association which in turn is based on the understanding of the ideograms.

Andre Leroi-Gourhan pointed out that in large-scale representations of animals during the Palaeolithic period in Europe, two animal species stand out; they are the bison and the horse that are often painted facing or close to each other and are accompanied by various recurring ideograms. Within the favourite theme, that of large-size wild animals, they are in their turn favourite subjects, which are repeated more often than others and this seems to explain something about the way associations are formed. There can be differences between one area and the other, put on the whole in the cave art of the French-Cantabrian area there are general characteristics whose possible conceptual meaning will be analysed later on.

In Tanzania, in the cave art of archaic hunters, the elephant and the giraffe play an associative role which is similar to that of the horse and the bison in Europe; indeed they often appear together and they are by far the most frequently represented animals. In the conceptuality of Tanzanian archaic hunters they probably play the same role that the horse and the bison had in French-Cantabrian conceptuality.

This idea paves the way for another paradigm, the presence in various groups of archaic hunters of dominating animal species have a dialectic relation with each other. The same model occurs in at least two regions. Western Europe and Tanzania between which no direct relations seem to have existed at the time the phenomenon took place. If we want to move from basic considerations about the phenomenon to the discovery of its meaning, it is necessary to have data concerning the remaining context, in particular, the associations with the ideograms, as well as systematic tests on the possible meanings of the ideograms themselves.

All this indicates the presence of paradigms: a detailed analysis might allow us to reach even further than we now imagine. The development of a systematic analysis to define the associations, composition and scenes, that is the kind of relations between one figure and the other in the same context, which represent the visual counterpart to the conceptual associative dynamic, seems particularly relevant. The first aim here is that of identifying models and constants, in order to define the terms of a phenomenology.

It has been noticed, for example, that in groups of developed hunters it is common to represent scenes, be they scenes of hunting, daily activities, worship or others, their range is rather limited. In groups of archaic hunters, no scenes describing proper episodes are represented, neither during the European Palaeolithic period or in other collections of cave art (or, if there are any, they have not yet been interpreted as such). There appear associations and compositions with a symbolic content, but apart from very rare exceptions no descriptive or narrative scenes have been found, which might lead to essential psychological elements.

There are also similar types of associations. In archaic hunters the spatial collocation of an animal within the framework of the other associated figures does not reflect naturalistic reality as our imagination today tends to see it for animal figures are placed on the wall in a repetitive way, on the basis of typologies which certainly had a meaning as a whole but do not reflect the kind of composition and the kind of vision common to our contemporary culture. It appears, for example, that in the art of archaic hunters the idea of "base" or treading ground was not very common. Apart from some rare exceptions, large animals are painted or engraved on the walls of caves as if they were levitating or floating in the air. The same happens in Europe as in Tanzania, Australia and elsewhere. People have often asked themselves whether these figures represented the animals proper or their "spirits" or if they had deeper meanings which we cannot grasp.

The association between animals and ideograms is represented with specific analogies by all archaic hunters. The animal figure is the subject, while the ideograms, the ones that Henri Breuil and Andre Leroi Gourhan called "symbols" are the reasoning around it. In populations of developed hunters, instead, scenic elements which indicate a completely different mentality can be found; according to our way of thinking the associations of developed hunters are more narrative, realistic and less abstract.

Sometimes the transition between the two forms is unforeseeable and may be at a certain moment the usual habits are abandoned to begin something new whereas in other instances there seems to be a gradual evolution and it is possible to indicate the transition phases. During these processes, changes in the cognitive mechanism begin to emerge.

A thematic analysis reveals the presence of groups of figure, signs and graphemes which represent what one might call the "vocabulary" of art and appear like words inside a sentence: but isolated signs are extremely rare, as isolated words are rare in speech. In art there are groups which reflect the association systems and represent the syntax: they are the "sentences" consisting of the grouping or sequence of graphemes. And this could be the key for the interpretation of prehistoric art, that is an ideography with universal characteristics, or anyway a series of constant associations which come before ethnic or linguistic borders. It seems possible therefore to postulate the existence of archetypal models of logic and this opens up interesting perspectives for the understanding of the human spirit. This is essentially the way to decode signs, not only of prehistoric art but, through the latter, of the basic elements of cognitive dynamics in our species.

If the isolated figures are analysed without seeing them in context, the result is a miscellaneous listing where the figure loses much of its meaning because it is separated from the rest. The truth is that these iconographic elements later undergo an exegesis, with subsequent interpretations not based on the whole but rather on some details, which may be striking but are taken out of context and consequently lead to incomplete interpretations. It is as if, in our language, we insisted on reading each word separately, thus refusing to see that there are sentences and that the words, apart from making grammatical sense, are joined together to construct clauses and sentences on the basis of syntactical logic.

Composite associations and cognitive accumulations that have formed over time often appear as well. Sometimes the process looks very complicated. On the wall of a cave, for example, one sees that at the beginning there were only three figures, two animals one in front of the other and an ideogram near them; a few generations later another figure was added and much later, may be after 2,000 years, other four signs were added. The panel shows us the end result where all these associations appear as part of a whole. It is necessary to identify the primary association, verify the repetitive elements, then compare the analogies and verify whether they are the result of casual or intentional overlapping.

In many cases there are some accumulations of signs which have constant features and are undoubtedly intentional, even though they may have been executed in different periods; others are not or we are simply unable to understand their meanings. It is therefore necessary to consider the accumulation of signs and figures onto the same surface.

In many cases the graphemes made by humans simply complete the natural shapes and colours which already existed on the background, by means of a similar cognitive process those who have added signs above or near the existing ones might sometimes have done it for similar purposes.

It has often been noticed that these figures express a real language of their own because there are widespread repetitive elements which must have been readable in all the places where they were made. Beyond the specific local characteristics found in Tanzania, in the decorated Palaeolithic caves in France or Spain and in the art of hunters in Australia or Patagonia, traces of this language which has its roots in the prototypes can be discovered.

Among these archetypal ideograms there are some very simple ones, some of which are universally widespread in all ages: the circle with a dot in the middle, the cross, the little stick, the line and dot, the "V" sign, the arrow, the roof-shape, the triangle, the square, the phallic and vulva signs, the five fingers, the series of parallel lines or of dots, the pair of circles. This primary categorization already contains enough elements to make up an "alphabet". Many signs are the same ones which, after having been used for thousands of years as ideograms in cave art, became part of the first ideographic writings, but which were also introduced as religious, philosophical or ideological concepts in various parts of the world.

The principles of a new methodology for comparative studies and for a wide contextual analysis of prehistoric art begin to emerge. It is now essential to collocate the fragmentary information available inside a system and to check to what extent the latter is applicable by verifying the presence of repetitive elements on a universal scale and which of these factors reflect contingent or local situations which are relevant only to the individual area.

It has already been noted that local elements become increasingly frequent as life gets more complicated, especially in groups with diversified or complex economies. In the art of hunters, universal paradigms prevail, obviously with variations and elements which still have to be understood. During prehistoric periods in Europe there are certainly no pictures of lamas and in Argentine no horses are represented, but on a universal scale animals are depicted on the basis of general criteria and not regarded as a species, given that animal species vary from one area to the other.

This shows us that there are universal cultural horizons on a global scale. Evidence of this is provided by the ideograms which repeat themselves because they are the same all over the world. For example, the print of the palm, both negative and positive, or the vulva and phallic symbols, the signs of crosses, sticks and trees which we find in European Palaeolithic art can be found in Tanzania as well as in America or Australia, within similar associations or contexts. These phenomena cannot be regarded as the manifestation of direct contact, but they presumably derive from a common cultural matrix.

The art of archaic hunters, then, appears to have universal features whereas the art of developed hunters has much more frequent local characteristics even though it maintains paradigms found worldwide. The real Babel Tower appears at the end of the hunting and gathering age. After this watershed, art, like many other aspects of culture, becomes increasingly provincial and is affected by contingent situations. The sequences of cave art found nearer to our modern culture thus becomes more understandable, while those found in other regions of the world appears increasingly exotic. There still are, however, countless common denominators, the first and most apparent of which being the need itself to produce stone art and furniture, the similar features, choice of subjects and kinds of associations. To these basic elements, which originated and developed already during the age of hunter clans, the fashions, styles, decorations and characteristics of the various tribes are added in more recent times.

The visual language of prehistoric art can probably be defined as an elementary language, so simple that it came to be used by groups of hunters all over the world tens of thousands of years back. It is frustrating for us, with our twentieth century technology, not to be able to understand it as clearly as our distant ancestors, who used it every day, must have been able to do.

It is possible to postulate that the universal primitive language is the same universal language we have inside us today and that, once we have found the key to it, it should be possible to reproduce it consciously. Indeed, we use it every day, although we are not fully aware of it; it contains the basic characteristics of logic and of the associative system, that are essential factors in the mechanisms of intuition, symbolization, conceptuality and rituals of the *Homo sapiens*. The conscious recovery of this language would allow us to understand each other beyond linguistic barriers because it is based on a primary logic, which comes before linguistic divisions and specialization. Theoretically this element should be contained in all languages and easily understandable by all of them. This would immediately lead us back to an understanding of the basic mechanisms of thought and logic as well as to the functioning of the basic associative mechanisms shared by all the people of the earth.

Rituals and Beliefs

The works of the first artists help us to reconstruct the intellectual roots of our species and even structural remains testify to the need for socialization of our "Sapiens" ancestors: in this way it is possible to rediscover their dwellings, meeting places, habits and daily needs.

The sites themselves, chosen by humans, where the artworks were executed—caves, shelters or rocky dens—often show a conceptual topography in which the place where the artworks are separated from the surrounding areas, but at the same time connected with them. In dark caves as in open-air stone art sites, the access to the engraved area has a function of transition and passage between two different "worlds". Still today human groups which produce stone art, such as the Nyau of Malawi in Africa or the aboriginals of the Arnhem Land in Australia, consider the engraved area as ceremonial and access to it is limited. Sometimes only the chosen few can enter them, in other cases access is granted only to members of one sex or only on certain occasions.

The stone art sites are often defined as "natural sanctuaries" unlike real sanctuaries (or artefacts) where at least parts of the shapes and structures are the intentional product of human work. The latter, made by the *Homo sapiens* more than 12,000 years ago, are extremely rare today as far as we know.

The oldest "sanctuary" known to date was discovered on a mountain in the Israeli Negev desert north of the Sinai peninsula and, judging by the chert tools found there, it probably dates back to more than 35,000 years ago. It is located in Har Karkom, a small half-hidden valley on the verge of a precipice and is known with the acronym HK/86B : it is surrounded by various settlements of the same age and overlooking the mountain, facing a wide view over valleys and hills up to the mountain chains, about 60 km to the east.

Har Karkom, a very important sacred mountain during the Bronze Age which became a large worship place, is located along one of the main trails which for time immemorial have linked Africa to Asia and the rest of the world (E. Anati, *Har Karkom in the Light of New Discoveries*, 1993). It also contains sources of excellent quality chert. This essential raw material during the Palaeolithic Age was extracted there even earlier and the excellent quality of the chert was probably one of the main reasons why humans chose this particular spot.

East of the sanctuary there is the precipice. From the borders of the sanctuary it is possible to see the hunting territory, the vast prairie below: on the other side the two peaks stand out, pointing at the sky like two breasts. Once you get there you see that one of them has, on the top, a small cave, while the other has a markedly phallic shape. It looks as if the landscape surrounding the site contained the male and female principles, as well as that of the complementarity between earth and sky, mountain and plain, dwelling and hunting area. The impression is that the landscape itself, with its shapes and topography, determined the location of the sanctuary.

About forty chert nodules, some of which are more than 1 metre tall, coming from three different quarries in an area of about 3 km have natural shapes reminding of the bust of humans, mostly females and animals. Once there, many people get the impression that it releases a powerful energy, the dark monoliths concentrated in a small valley on the verge of a precipice and the surrounding lunar landscape create a breathtaking landscape architecture.

Some of these natural statues weigh several hundred kilos; a large effort must have been necessary to carry them there. They have been grouped in the central area and some of them have been shaped by men. On a surface area of about 400 square metres, apart from the numerous worked cherts, about 220 chert pebbles with anthropomorphic and zoomorphic shapes with occasional touches have been found; their size ranges between 35 and 5 cm and they weigh up to 20 kg. There are also glyptoliths and lines of pebbles which form drawings on the fossil soil.

The function of this site is not completely clear. It is neither a dwelling site nor does it seem to have played an economic role. It was definitely a meeting place with nature and probably also an area of meditation on the alchemy of nature. This is probably the place where humans tried to understand the meaning of natural shapes, from the pebbles that were collected here and from the surrounding view.

This sanctuary has three main characteristics. It is an excellent observation point from which it is possible to control the hunting area below as if it were a meeting point with nature with its mountain tops on one side and vast plains on the other; it also shows a particular interest for the natural shape of the stones and indicates that humans used to collect and organize stones having natural anthropomorphic and zoomorphic shapes. The association between these two shapes, human and animal, which captured the interest of Palaeolithic men, will be an essential element in the art and conceptuality of the *Homo sapiens* for the following 25,000 years. It can also be found in funeral figures in Siberia, in open-air rock art and in the sanctuary-caves, as well as in the stone art of the hunters of all the continents inhabited by humans. Around the sanctuary, there are various dwelling sites with hut pavings which are still clearly visible with remains of fireplaces, areas for chert cutting and numerous stone tools.

Another Palaeolithic sanctuary, 20,000 years younger than the one in Har Karkom has been found in the El-Juyo cave, in the Cantabrian area of Spain. Researchers L. Freeman and R. Klein (1983) describe what they define as a temple dating back to fourteen thousand years ago. Inside it they found a room with a pile of stones, which they called "altar", and a stone with two facets: anthropomorphic on one side and zoomorphic on the other. The association between humans and beasts appears once again: this is a recurring element in Palaeolithic art where, apart from the associations mentioned above, there are also images of anthropo-zoomorphic beings.

The room was presumably a meeting place in which the pile with the anthropo-zoomorphic stone must have played an essential role. The symbiosis between humans and animals was a common syntactic formula and may be it evoked a story of real life, an original myth or a strong conceptual reference.

Like the sanctuary of Har Karkom, this also appears to have been a meeting or reunion place, with an icon provided by a stone with a natural shape which was collected by men and put in a special position. In this specific case, the stone was placed on top of a heap, while in Har Karkom the larger orthostats were placed vertically.

Other Palaeolithic sites have been interpreted as sanctuaries, but their fragmentary preservation state raises doubts about their possible identification. At Gonnersdorf, in the Rhine Valley in Germany, G. Bosinsky (1970) found a paleosoil in which holes have been escavated. The latter contained partly broken tablets with engravings of female and animal silhouettes, in an order which seems to suggest a ritualistic behaviour towards these images. Here again there had been an interplay between animal and human figures. The icons in this case were not permanently exhibited, but had been buried inside the holes presumably during a celebration. In various caves, some of which contain rock art, archaeological layers with tablets and anthropomorphic figures have been found, but no structure of considerable size could be connected to the figures themselves.

What happened inside these sanctuaries which appear as collections of artistic manufacts? This question has been asked very often but no satisfactory answer has been given yet. We can only guess, by comparing the similar sanctuaries built by contemporary tribal populations, that they were places of initiation, meditation, transmission of traditions and myths. The celebrations, in ethnologic contexts, are linked with these functions.

In the case of the HK/86B sanctuary of Har Karkom in particular, a lot of energy must have been devoted to the installation of the works, monoliths, glyptoliths, anthropomorphic and zoomorphic pebbles. What was the drive and the motivation behind this behaviour? Was it planned beforehand? Was there a coordination, were there priests involved, and special events during which these celebrations took place? All of these questions still go unanswered and remain on a theoretical level, but something can be said, however. In Har Karkom and in the other sanctuaries, some main areas of concern seem to emerge: the exploration and understanding of nature, of the meaning of natural shapes, of human-animal and human-environment relations.

In the religion and philosophy of Upper Palaeolithic men a dualistic vision of the universe appears, which is revealed in these sanctuaries and also becomes apparent in many other manifestations of artistic creativity.

Some aspects of this conceptuality in Palaeolithic art had already been revealed through research carried out by Andre Leroi-Gourhan and Annette Laming Emperaire more than 25 years ago (A. Laming Emperaire, *Art rupestre Paleolithique*, 1962: A. Leroi-Gourhan, *Prehistoire Art Occidental*, 1965). It has been suggested that Palaeolithic artists gave masculine and feminine connotations to the various animals, objects and symbols they represented: today the phenomena observed seem to indicate not so much a sexual definition but rather a dualistic conception.

Symbolism and Intellect

In the world depicted by the fossil of *Homo sapiens* it seems that all existing elements had their counterpart, that everything consisted of two halves which complemented one another in the same way expressed today by a spouse when talking about the other "half". The female half needed the other male half to function biologically and to be itself, and vice versa. Man and woman, the human and animal world, earth and sky, light and darkness, night and day, the dark cave and the outside world, everything was divided into two divisions and completeness resulted from the union of the two complementary sides. The question is how this philosophy developed. It is an extremely complex question and we shall attempt to simplify it, even though this involves the risk of providing partial and inevitably schematic explanations.

Many of the archaeological findings, which apart from the artworks include burial and worship places, remains of dwellings and camps and numerous tools for daily use, seem to indicate that ever since humans started to develop their capacity for abstraction, synthesis and complex association, their two main concerns have been with life and death. An oriental proverb goes: "Death is the fulfilment of life", without life there is no death and without death there is no life.

The death of a member of the species is a traumatic experience also for many animals; the awareness of one's mortality came later and is still refused today by some archaeologists. The cult of the dead as we have seen, appears to have been an invention of Neanderthal men, who lived between 1,00,000 and 35,000 years ago and created the Musterian material culture. It was then conceived in a much more elaborate way by the *Homo sapiens*.

In Europe, up to the beginning of the Upper Palaeolithic period about 35,000 years ago, the cult of the dead was often a way of celebrating life in the first place. Painting (spreading) the dead with okra paint, giving them the colour of blood or supplying them with food, are acts which express life rather than death. We discover that, in the primitive conceptuality of humans, life and death were seen as a complementary couple. This is also shown by the vulva images (symbols of life) on the body of figures representing animal preys (that is animals which were killed and used as food) in Tito Bustillo and other caves in the French-Cantabrian area (A. Beltran, *BCSP*, vol. 24, 1988). The dualistic indivisibility of life and death emerges here.

Survival was ensured mainly by hunting, which is why an existential relationship started between humans and animals. For humans life had more or less the same meaning that the "soul" has in western conceptuality today; animal life nourished human life. Today we are pleased to know, how many proteins we eat, or, more simply, by feeling "full up". Then, as today, humans felt satisfied after they had eaten. What is considered a physical satisfaction by people today, must have provided our ancestors with the sensation of having acquired the strength of the animal whose meat they had eaten. The meal was the means through which the spiritual symbiosis which led to completeness was fulfilled and became a reality with the integration of the spirit of the animal inside the body of humans. Some populations of hunters maintain these beliefs, which are improperly called "animistic" still today (C.P. Mountford, *Art, Myth and Symbolism*, 1956). The frequent cases of representations of humans disguised as animals or of anthropo-zoomorphic hybrid figures in the art of archaic hunters dramatically demonstrates this search for a symbiosis.

Hunters' populations had developed a dual relation between humans and animals: the hunted animals were identified with survival, the live animals were a symbol of vitality: here the concept of a life-death relation appears again. Through the physical assimilation of the animal's meat, its strength, vitality and real or alleged skills were acquired as well. The hunters felt revitalized, much more than in a physical sense by this customary act of eating, which acquired what we today would call a "mystic" significance. The meal was an act of communion, which was practised almost daily, between the animal and the human world or, in a more generic sense, between humans and the surrounding world, those who take and those who give. In some contemporary religions there are residues of similar concepts, especially in the ritual meals, real or symbolic, which are taken.

Hunting was planned and rational. There had to be very strict rules on the subject, maybe similar to those found today among the Lapps, Eskimos, Boscimans, Sandawe, Hazda, Aranda and other populations of hunters in the five continents. Some of these rules, with minor variations, are still widespread all over the world in these populations.

The aim of these norms is not to jeopardize the continuity of the hunted species which constituted the reserve, safety and therefore the heritage of the territory and of the clan. Females and young animals were never killed. Those animals were selected which had already completed their life cycle and whose extinction did not upset the further development of the animal world. This shows another aspect of the dual attitude of humans towards animals; the latter were in some cases regarded as preys to be killed, other times to be left untouched in order to safeguard the necessary balance that would ensure the preservation of the resources. The application of the dualistic concept to the human-animal relation continues in totemic visions of nature still common among contemporary tribal populations.

Another essential element for survival was the relation between man and woman which ensured the fulfilment of natural biological needs, as well as the preservation of the species. The sexual act of communion also had a revitalizing and strengthening function which contributed to the stability of the social structure as well as to the sense of harmony and comfort. We still do not know to what extent these peoples were aware of paternity; there are still tribes where the relation between sex and pregnancy is not understood. The biological need of copulating, however, is certainly not a human invention and the dualistic man-woman perception remains an essential conceptual factor up until the present day.

In the light of these clear examples of complementary couples as factors of completeness and unity, it is easy to understand how the concept of dualism or bipolarism developed and extended to other aspects of the beliefs and visions of the universe. According to this view, each of the two poles needed the other to fulfill itself, as in the case of electric charges with opposite signs which, by touching each other, produce sparks. A very similar conceptuality still existed among some Australian tribes when Charles Mountford studied them in the 1940s.

Indeed, Palaeolithic art seems to reflect this dualism in a surprisingly complex fashion. Its representations include animals with a "male" and a "female" meaning. In the decorated caves of France and Spain, for example, images of horses and bisons are associated. According to the interpretation given by A. Leroi-Gourhan, the horse in front of the bison is an expression of this dualistic concept. For the hunter clans of the prairie or of the savannah, the agile, slender and fast horse is a male symbol, while the plump, slow and pensive bison represents femininity. We have already seen how, in Tanzania, similar roles are played by the giraffe and by the elephant. The animals change, but the ideas remain the same.

In the Palaeolithic sanctuary of Har Karkom the dualistic meaning of the landscapes, the symbolism of natural shapes and the dualistic relations between humans and environment, humans and animals, earth and sky all emerge very powerfully.

In the cosmogonic vision which was maintained by philosophies of later ages, earth (feminine) and sky (masculine) were regarded as a pair formed by two halves, one male and one female. The same can be applied to sea (masculine) and land (feminine), sun (masculine) and moon (feminine). Many elements of Palaeolithic conceptuality are not only present in some contemporary populations of hunters, but also latent in our subconscious: we rediscover them once they emerge. It should also be pointed out that the masculine or feminine gender attributed to some elements which would be considered neutral by contemporary logic standards, has been kept in some modern languages, such as Italian and French, and is probably a residue of the "animistic" conception according to which they were considered.

The hunting men of the Palaeolithic period had probably created an image of the universe which was affected by their functional relation with the animal world; the wonderful art of the sanctuary-caves exalts these aspects of conceptuality and spirituality. The meeting of bison and horse on cave paintings, as in the prairie environment, hid the messages of a deep reality which symbolized the universe.

The repetitive system of pictograms, ideograms and psychograms which humans used in their conceptual applications uses detail by giving it a symbolic value for what is general, while contingent aspects are transformed into a symbol of universality. In this way, the horse and the bison had meanings which went much beyond the purely figurative value we attribute to them today; their association in cave art added further meanings to the whole and the ideograms accompanying them each contained their own messages.

All these graphic expressions derive from the details gathered by observing the world. Humans used daily reality to enrich their intelligence, fighting with the enormous animals they depicted, mammoths, bisons, horses, bulls, rhinoceros, was exciting. The cosmological concept was associated with a mythology full of imagination and ingeniousness which inspired sublime works of art. The latter represent the effect and today archaeologists look into their causes.

Now the question emerges of the relation between the findings, its study and the cultural acquisition of its meaning. It is not enough for a finding to cause a response of aesthetic apprecia-tion for it to be accepted as part of the culture; people today, as they did yesterday, require contents and when faced with a message they might accept or reject it. On the other hand, if there is no message there is nothing to understand. The picture of a bison or mammoth painted on the wall of a cave can look beautiful or ugly, but it is only by discovering its meaning that it becomes a cultural artefact. Over the past few years archaeology has made giant leaps towards the understanding of contents and we are probably now facing a turning-point from where research might lead us to the discovery of the universal processes of the human brain.

The discovery of meaning raises several questions, as indeed the dualistic concept of hunters populations is still very much part of our way of thinking, it belongs to our "logic" so that, thousands of years later, we can still define as "truth" the principles expressed by Palaeolithic conceptuality. For us it appears "obvious" that death should be the completion of life, that man complements woman and vice versa and that night should follow day, there is no question of believing these concepts or refusing them because they reflect our natural way of thinking. This is true for Buddhists as well as for Christians and it continues to be a universal element of human conceptuality.

What is expressed by primitive visual language is a conceptual world which reflects a certain *forma mentis*, a frame of mind. It contains intellectual speculations, beliefs, myths, it allows to discover traditions and rites which have characterized human existence for thousands of years. The preservation of these associations over hundreds of generations leads to think that there was an absolute and complete faith in this cosmological vision, a faith which sustained humanity from 40,000 to about 10,000 years ago. An ideology based on the epic celebration of dualism, expressed by the daily confrontation between humans and animals which became the basis of analogies for other comparisons: between man and woman, night and day, light and darkness, earth and sky, life and death, the reality of being awake and dreaming. This intellectual-religious world is being brought back to the level of consciousness by the comparative study of similar art forms and concepts present in many hunters populations which still inhabit the remotest corners of the earth. It reveals to us the wonderful magic of human intelligence, an essential feature of our species ever since its origins.

Conclusion

At the end of the Palaeolithic period, an unexpected phenomenon took place in the Euro-Asiatic regions under the form of a sudden climatic change. Its cause is not known yet, but various hypotheses have been made about it. This environmental upheaval called "universal flood" by many mythologies, brought about some radical transformations.

As the glaciers melted, the large plains were invaded by water, millions of tons of ice from the mountains and the widest areas of the Arctic region started to melt and turned the plains into lakes and marshes: the sea level rose by about 120 metres so that immense expansions of land and probably thousands of human groups went under. The Persian Gulf, for example, was an enclosed sea much smaller than it is now; the rising in the sea level flooded the plains where the rivers Tigris and Euphrates flowed further south for many miles. The northern half of the Adriatic sea was a wide plain, an ideal habitat for hunter clans and their preys; the Maltese archipelago was an extension of Sicily and the latter was a peninsula. The shores of the Mediterranean went back more than 100 kilometres in some points and the sea covered the prairies. Australia was joined with New Zealand and the Beiring Straits were accessible. Changes in the ecosystem took place almost everywhere: most of Canada, once free of ice, could be inhabited, the Sahara received abundant rain and for several thousand years it became a sort of paradise where populations of hunters and gatherers produced wonderful artworks.

In Europe, which had a mild climate, animals were totally integrated with their environment, they survived on an animal and vegetable diet from the tundra and undergrowth, built up a food chain and adapted to the cold dry climate. After the climate changes that accompanied the "universal flood", the tundra disappeared and some animals, like the mammoth that were too integrated to be able to change their habits, became extinct. On the other hand, others, like the deer and the chamois, abandoned the plains and easily adapted to the mountain environment and have therefore survived up to the present day.

Those human groups which were not exterminated by this "universal flood" had to change their diet in order to survive, and started to hunt small animals, such as hares, aquatic animals and wild ducks. This brought about radical changes in human life, social structures and intellectual concepts. Earlier, if you depended on mammoth meat, it was not economical to live in small family groups because you went hunting in large groups which were able to carry hundreds of kilos of meat back to the camp and many people shared the meat. If your diet consisted of ducks or hares, the hunting system changes, as the economy and the size of the group itself is transformed. Still today people use different associations when they think about the mammoth (large industry) and about a rabbit (the Playboy club). Even in contemporary hunter populations there are different social and behavioural models for hunters of large animals (or large-scale fauna) and hunters of small-scale animals.

When the animals changed, after the climatic mutations at the end of the Pleistocene, human groups adapted to the new situation. Archaeological digging show different characteristics if compared to the previous dwellings of the Palaeolithic and the following ones of the Mesolithic age. During the Mesolithic period in Europe, remains of human dwellings inside small caves are usually found, with a small fireplace, the remains of shellfish and other small and medium-size animals. The Palaeolithic camp, on the other hand, is often characterized by the presence of large fireplaces and many bones of large animals. A series of observations made about these findings reveal that, at the end of the Palaeolithic period in Europe, in some cases a transformation in the social structure took place; the clan was divided into family groups which went to inhabit areas, one distant from the other because each one needed its own hunting territory. Previously a substantial group of adults hunted large animals, whose meat was then carried to the camp and shared; thirty Mesolithic hunters, on the other hand, did not go hunting, thirty rabbits in the same area; every group took care of itself. It seems that the particular family structure of our European society originated during the Mesolithic period and brought with it a new concept of social aggregation.

Another aspect of the traumatic effect of the changes in climate is more ideological. The absolute truth summed up by the dualistic concept, the faith in that philosophy which had survived for 30,000 years and seemed eternal and unshakeable, suddenly did not seem to make sense any longer because its main elements, the epic of the fight between humans and large animals, failed. In this way a faith, which had survived for a period of fifteen times longer than the time which separates us from the beginning of our era, suddenly collapsed.

The sanctuary caves of the French-Cantabrian area with their wonderful paintings were abandoned; even though they remained the same, with their own characteristics, they no longer had a reason to be preserved. It is not by chance that we rediscover and begin to appreciate them in our age today, after 10,000 years of oblivion. This also gives some hints about our own era.

As a consequence of external environmental factors, the absolute truth, the universal religion, suddenly broke down and humans found themselves caught up in a spiritual void. It took them several thousand years to build back an ideology of their own, after undergoing a period of disappointing intellectual expressivity during the Mesolithic period. There are rare and schematic expressions also in the area of visual language, apart from the regions where humans maintained a decadent Palaeolithic tradition, also known as Epipaleolithic, presumably with remains of an archaic religion which did not make much sense in the new situation.

In Valcamonica, the Protocamune period, with large-scale animal figures (the elks found in Luine) is an Epipaleolithic expression, that is a late and decadent Palaeolithic manifestation of a marginal group which, almost driven by inertia, continued the Palaeolithic tradition during the Mesolithic period in a disorganized way, without the wealth of ideographic associations and the profound philosophical contents which had characterized cave art (E. Anati, *The Camunes*, 1982).

Only during the eighth and seventh millennium B.C. following great technological developments, the invention of new tools, the first experiences in working the land and breeding animals, did humans in Europe and the Near East enter a new "renaissance" stage which enabled them to create a new ideology and to start their intellectual reconstruction. From the Neolithic period onwards, it is possible to follow the conceptual evolution of the European and Middle Eastern world which led to the present day. The basic formulas have been largely undermined by more complex overlapping; sometimes the ability to synthesize has not been able to handle new conceptual problems and it is during these times that a taste for the ephemeral emerges.

The story of the other continents is rather different. In those happy parts of the planet such as Australia, as well as most of Africa and South America, where living conditions and natural resources have not undergone radical modifications, there have been no grounds for substantial changes in lifestyle. In other areas, including large parts of continental Asia and the Middle East, lush prairies became deserts and humans left them to move somewhere else, thus leaving wide areas in the dry regions as a shelter for weaker populations and outcast groups, doomed to lead a dire life.

Strangely enough, it is in these dry areas inhabited by outcast populations that we find the largest concentration of artistic creativity, vast sites of stone art with hundreds of thousands of figures. Twelve thousand years ago the whole of humanity survived by hunting and gathering, the economy and the social structure started to diversify with the origin and development of pastoral and agricultural populations with a complex economy. Art reflects these changes and shows us the variety of forms and concepts which have been constantly growing over the centuries.

This evolution provides us with a series of data which allows us to reflect on the anatomy of the human adventure. History never repeats itself in the same way, but the past is inside us; experiences, achievements and even failures enrich our conceptual wealth. The resulting discoveries are part of the heritage which nothing can take away from us.

9

Anthropology, Proteins and DNA: Molecules as a Tool in the Reconstruction of Human Evolution

Giovanni Destro-Bisol

The persistence of the chemical blood relationships between the various groups of animals serves to carry us back into geological times, and I believe that it will lead to valuable results in the study of various problems of evolution.

—*Nuttall (1904)*[1]

The Anthropometric Variables and the Impact of "Geography" on Human Evolution

Starting off from an every day perception, that of the extreme range of variability in the people we meet, we can try to outline which elements determine this "diversity", skin or eye colour, height, or nose shape can easily be pointed out. Using these traits, we can place individuals in "categories" like Whites or Blacks, tall and short. Starting from a simple perception, we have moved towards a more rational formulation, even if a simple and purely descriptive one. If this level still does not satisfy us, the next step is that of analysing the causes of such diversity: the attempt to write our evolutionary history: the set of processes responsible for the biological variation of the species, in space and time.

Through the observation and analysis of the final results of biological variation in space and time, we have reached an interpretative approach, in which our ability to reconstruct the evolutionary phenomena is fundamental. Since it is not feasible to take into account all available biological traits, we can operate a selection: one way, is to use a set of variables which, like skin colour or height, measure the physical shapes and sizes of the external components of the human body (anthropometric traits), and are hence easily accessible and surveyable. In this way, we have formulated a working hypothesis, which apart from a correct intuition, carries some limitations. By placing in their biological context the signs of evolutionary processes, anthropometric traits can in fact provide us with important information regarding our past. However, in a historical reconstruction, the biological component of greatest interest is the genetic one, that is, one which is transmitted (almost) unaltered from a generation to the other, spanning between evolutionary past and present. The limitations follow. The display of anthropometric traits which we observe (phenotype) is the result of the combined action between polygenetic and environmental factors, a circumstance which raises difficulties in decoding the genetic information. Having solved this first drawback, we face yet another problem: anthropometric traits physically relate man to the environment, which can influence his geographical distribution through natural selection: it suffices to think of the significance of the skin's hyperpigmentation in populations in areas with high solar radiation or to the particular body size (with growth of the thorax and shortening of the limbs) which protects Eskimos from heat dispersal.

Let us take a closer look at how disagreement can be created between evolutionary history and the evolution of biological structures. Some readers may be familiar with the surprising resemblance of the octopus and man's eye, one of the classical examples of evolutionary convergence. This particular similarity between two unquestionably distant species certainly does not indicate of them having a common history, it rather underlines how analogies in functional requirements, imposed by the environment, have brought evolution to select similar features. We must then consider the opposite case: two populations separated in relatively recent times, settled in very different ecological contexts, can undergo a great differentiation of those traits influenced by the interaction with the environment.

The most evident examples of disagreement between a specie's global evolution and that of certain particular traits arise from the comparison between different species. The evolution of human anthropometric variables suffers from analogous phenomena, even if their effect is considerably reduced both by capacity of adaptation on a cultural basis and by the considerable possibility of genetic admixture.

In sum, the biological information we can obtain from anthropometric traits ends up by having relevance not only with the "history" but also with the "geography" of human evolution. An exclusively anthropometric approach may hence be unsatisfactory to our purpose.

Which other Traits, for the Reconstruction of the Evolutionary History?

Given that our goal is that of specifically analysing the historical component of human evolution, can we still draw from the biological differentiation of our species as a source of information? An answer comes from the French molecular Biologist Francois Jacob,[2] who asserts that complex objects (and hence biological diversity) are:

> ... produced by evolutionary processes in which two factors are paramount, the constraints that at every level control the systems are involved, and the historical circumstances that control the actual interactions between the systems.

To avoid falling in the limitations of the anthropometric traits, we should select appropriate working tools, exempt from the action of natural selection (and therefore "neutral"), provided with known physio-chemical properties and with a simple and predictable genetic transmission. In this way, it should be easier to obtain genetic information to which rigorous and suitable mathematical models can be applied. We have in this way traced a profile corresponding to both proteins and DNA.

Having satisfied our first query, we can try to clarify the relation between molecules and evolutionary history as at this point we need to introduce the concept of genetic polymorphism.

Genetic Polymorphisms

In the first decade of this century, some scholars, amongst whom the Austrian immunologist Karl Landsteiner, have highlighted the possibility of distributing individuals of a population in (blood-) groups based on the immunological reactions between their erythrocytes and other individuals serum. Successive researches have demonstrated that at the base of this immunological phenomena there are structural differences among the glycoproteins which constitute certain antigens of the erythrocyte membrane (ABO, Rh and Lewis systems). It has also been demonstrated that group-specific traits are transmitted from a generation to the other according to the patterns described by Gregor Mendel in 1886. Landsteiner's blood groups represent the first examples of genetic polymorphisms, that is, the condition in which the same protein can present variable aminoacidic sequence from an individual to another, and that each variant can be under genetic control.

Unlike anthropometric variables, genetic polymorphisms are generally under control of single genes, whose expression produces phenotypes unaffected from the environments influence. The same genetic variability generally unfolds in a limited number of well differentiated variants, easing both the scoring of genetic traits and their statistical analysis. All these properties make it easy to retrace the genetic traits of each individual from his phenotype.

Thanks to the knowledge of the physio-pathological implications of genetic polymorphisms, it is possible to distinguish those genetic polymorphisms whose distribution is driven by natural selection (e.g., anomalous haemoglobins and thalassemia which have an adaptive significance with respect to malaria) from the substantially neutral ones. Basing themselves on the latter, population geneticists have developed theoretical models for the evaluation of genetic relationships between groups, and for the analysis of those phenomena (isolation, inbreeding, migrations) which determine how genes assort themselves in the population (genetic structure). The availability of new methodologies and dedicated interpretative models gave birth in the sixties to a new area of research conventionally referred to as "genetic anthropology".

When an important methodological renewal arises in a scientific discipline, its conceptual contents end up being profoundly influenced. In anthropology's case, this is clearly illustrated by the revision of the biological concept of race in the second half of our century.[3]

From Race to Population: The Birth of Evolutionary Anthropology

The interpretation of biological diversity in humans, on a typological basis, began to impose itself in the nineteenth century. In line with this approach, several anthropologists began to use height, degree of pigmentation or other anthropometric traits to group individuals in discrete and immutable entities: the "races". Under the influence of the social and cultural climate, in some cases, intellectual capacities and psychic qualities have ended up by being associated with racial classification, up to the appearance of unfounded theories like that of the "purity of the race" or "Aryan race", in the first decade of the twentieth century.

One must wait for the definite defeat of the totalitarian regimes in the second half of our century for the social and political typological concept of race to be finally reconsidered. With regards to the scientific sphere, two events concurred decisively to this change: the introduction of several genetic polymorphisms and the development of population genetics, which provided valuable methods and models for the interpretation of genetic viability. Concisely, there are two evidences which are clearly in disfavour of the scientific validity of the concept of race: (i) it has been observed that more than 90 per cent of genetic variability is in no way dependent on any racial classification; (ii) using different genetic polymorphisms and/or morphometric traits, different evolutionary reconstructions have been obtained (phylogenetic trees), in evident disagreement between them.

In sum, genetic polymorphisms have significantly contributed to an important change in our discipline, thanks to which anthropologists have understood the opportunity of trying to understand the dynamic processes which are at the base of biological diversity, rather than using it for the construction of racial classification. With the decline of the concept of race, the role as evolutionary unit has been ascribed to the population; aggregate of individuals which actually exchange their genes not only because they share a geographical area, but also a cultural and social history. The grounds are thus prepared, for the development of a discipline which fully deserves the definition of evolutionary anthropology.

At the Origins of Genetic Variability : DNA's Polymorphisms

During the seventies, anthropologists' and population geneticists' attention has begun to shift from the product of genetic information's translation (the proteins), to the very object in which such information resides; DNA. In the course of about fifteen years, DNA's polymorphisms have in many cases ended up by substituting those at protein level. The noteworthy effort which has brought this profound methodological renewal has been abundantly compensated by the advantages.

In the first place, one must consider that a considerable part of DNA is not transcribed at all in messenger RNA (non-coding DNA) and that a portion of the transcript is not even translated into aminoacids. All these "silent" components of the genetic material, like the processes that determined their evolution, can be detected only by directly analysing the DNA.

Apart from obtaining a greater quantity of information, there is the possibility to adapt investigation strategies in relation to the specific genetic components or evolutionary problems which one intends to analyse: while protein polymorphisms and DNA autosomic loci identify traits which derive from the combination of the two parents mendelian traits, the analysis of mitochondrial DNA and that of non-recombining portions of the Y-chromosome allow us to follow the evolution of the genetic traits exclusively by maternal (mt DNA) or paternal (Y-chromosome) lineage.

The last substantial advantages come from the possibility to choose one or another region of DNA according to its 'temporal scale'. The coding and regulative portions, and the proteins translated alike, undergo stringent functional constraints which discard harmful mutations, limiting the rate of evolution. In these conditions, the information relative to phylogenetically remote events can be maintained with greater ease (e.g., the separation between human and other primates lineages). A somewhat opposite situation is presented by those regions which do not take part in protein synthesis: free from evolutionary constraints, these regions can evolve faster and accumulate mutations in a relatively brief time span. In the latter case, important information regarding relatively recent processes of genetic differentiation between populations can be obtained.

The Past through the Future: The Neontological Approach

I hope that at this point the reasons why proteins and DNA represent important tools for the reconstruction of the evolutionary history of our species are sufficiently clear to the reader. Now, to better focus on the potential and limits of the bio-molecular approach, we can use as terms of comparison another, perhaps more familiar area of anthropological research, that of Paleoanthropology (see also G. Manzi's article in this volume).

In the paleoanthropological approach, the material under study constitutes generally in parts of fossilized skeletons, with which one tries to reconstruct the morphological traits of one or more individuals. In some cases, even a single finding can be of extraordinary importance. In the bio-molecular approach, the analysis is instead based on samples of individuals, large enough to be representative of the population to whom they belong. Leaving a mark in the populations "gene pool", are not morphological traits, but admixture, migrations, expansions and reductions in population size: by analysing the way in which the genes are combined in present human groups, we can thus try to reconstruct demographic events. The most surprising aspect of this "neontological" approach is perhaps the fact that even extremely distant events, like those which brought the appearance of the human lineage first, the affirmation of *Homo sapiens* successively, can be reconstructed on the basis of the genetic variability belonging to groups presently populating our planet.

The Molecular Clock and the Origins of Modern Man

In this brief review, the importance of theoretical models for the interpretation, the genetic data in evolutionary terms have several times been recalled and they generally imply extremely complex formulations, but one of these lend itself to a brief description even here: the molecular clock model.

In part of our hereditary material (cells of the germinal line), single base mutations tend to occur with a presumably constant rate; mutations which do not affect the individuals' reproductive and survival expectations (fitness), are the most apt for the construction of the molecular clock. The total number of different sites which single base mutations dispose of is so large (about 3 thousand million nucleotides in nuclear DNA, 16500 in mitocondrial DNA) that it is virtually impossible for independent mutational events to result into identical genetic changes.

In gathering all these elements, it may be understood that the genetic differences between individuals tend to accumulate in function of time. It derives that genetic diversity within a population can reflect its age, while the differences between species, or even between two populations in reciprocal geographical isolation can carry indications on the time span occurred since their separation from the parental species, or population.

One of the best known applications of the molecular clock is that regarding the origin of modern man. According to the hypothesis backed by some Paleoanthropologists and Geneticists (see G. Manzi's contribution to this same volume), anatomically modern man appeared in sub-Saharan Africa in relatively recent times (between 100,000 and 500,000 years ago), from where he diffused in other geographical areas. One of the most important genetical implications of this hypothesis is that Africans,* by constituting the most ancient group, carry in their DNA more mutations than Europeans and Asians do.[4] In fact, the majority of bio-molecular data collected so far agree in indicating the greatest diversity to be within Africans. Estimates regarding the time of appearance and expansion of ancestral populations, realized through the analysis of DNA, strengthen the idea that this feature is to be related to the form of evolution proposed by the "African origin" hypothesis of anatomically modern man.[5]

The New Frontiers: The Paleogenetics

The possibility of characterizing of DNA from fossil and mummified remains surely consists in one of the aspects of evolutionary research which most attracts the widest interest from

---

* For brevity, the term "Africans" is used in relation to the sub-Saharan populations of Africa.

the public.[6] Apart from purely fairy-tale aspects (like that of recreating dinosaurs or other extinct animals in lab), the development of "paleogenetics" has opened new prospects in the study of evolutionary biology.

For the birth of Paleogenetics, the role of methodological advances has been fundamental too. DNA which is extracted from ancient remains is in fact extremely degraded by bacterial restriction enzymes, precluding or raising difficulties in its characterization with traditional bio-molecular techniques. For this reason this field of research has only effectively begun to develop from the end of the eighties, thanks to the introduction of the Polymerase Chain Reaction (PCR). This technique allows to obtain copies of specific DNA fragments even in conditions of extreme degradation. Once "amplified" the specific DNA fragments can easily be analysed by determining their nucleotide sequence or more simply by measuring their size by electrophoretic techniques.*

A first significant step anthropologists are taking is that of analysing the genetic affinity between extant and present populations from the same geographical area,[7] integrating and placing side by side the data obtained from the traditional morphometric traits with that from genetic and protein polymorphisms. In this case, the interest in reconstructing evolutionary sequences based on first hand data (rather than using theoretical models, however valid and rigorous) is straightforward. The most suggestive prospect offered by Paleogenetics is undoubtedly that of determining on a molecular base the degree of relationship between "key" fossil findings, until now analysed solely on a morphological base.

Biological and Cultural Evolution: The Interdisciplinary Approach

Amongst the questions with which I opened this brief review, one I haven't answered so far regards the difficulties that can arise from the evolutionary reconstructions based on the interaction

---

* Electrophoresis is based on the molecule's capacity to migrate in a porous support, immersed in buffer solution, to which a potential difference is applied. With this technique, the number of bases which compose a given fragment of DNA can be determined, since the migration rate of the molecules in the electrophoretic support, depends on their size.

between biological and cultural factors. To tackle this point, we can resort to an example: the genetic history of Italy, as proposed by Alberto Piazza et al.[8], in 1988, which is an interesting application of genetic Anthropology to problems related to peopling. Using data relevant to six different genetic polymorphisms (for a total of 40 variants). Piazza and collaborators have constructed synthetic maps in which genetic variability is synthesized, and transposed on geographical map. From this analysis, certain zones of genetic differentiation emerge, amongst which one in southern Italy, and another in central Italy. Combining genetic data with linguistic knowledge and historical-demographic reconstructions, an interesting relation results between certain genetic aspects emerged from the synthetic maps and from peopling events preceding the achievement of the Roman Empire: the first area of differentiation finds correspondence with the so-called Magna Grecia area, and coherently, the genetic structure results are similar to that of modern Greece: the second area is instead superimposable with the area corresponding to the Etruskean's distribution. The suggestive conclusion is that ancient events, such as the colonization of southern Italy by the Greeks or the occupation of central Italy by the Etruskeans, are responsible for a consistent part of present day Italian population's genetic structure.

As illustrated by Piazza and collaborators' work, the integration among anthropological, archaeological, linguistic and demographic data, has permitted to formulate important theories on the processes of peopling of key areas for the origin of cultures in pre and prohistorical times. In addition to the previous example, it is worth reminding the hypothesis by Cavalli-Sorza and Ammermann,[9] according to which the first agricultural practises would have diffused in Europe starting from nearly 8000 years ago, through migratory waves of populations moving from Anatolia (see also the work apported by G. Barbujani in this same volume).

The Future of Anthropology between Evolutionary Complexity and Methodological Diversity

With this short review, I have tried to bring the readers' attention to what can be considered two amongst the most important factors for the development of our discipline. We first saw that the possibility of analysing genetic variability directly at DNA level opens new and important perspectives for Anthropology. It has then been highlighted how the possibility of integration between different lines of evidence, both biological and cultural, can accord bio-molecular's inherently redactive approach with the more complex evolutionary phenomena in which the biological component often interacts with the cultural one.

Despite these important leads in development, the path Anthropology needs to read is undoubtedly still a long one. According to some researchers, the path to strike to answer many of the unsolved problems in the field of human evolution is, above all, one of methodological innovations.

> *Think of what we could deduce if we knew the DNA base-pair of every human now alive. We could reconstruct much of the history of human populations in terms of prehistoric migrations, and founder effect. We could study the social structure of human populations, the frequencies and types of mutations, and natural selection in humans along environmental gradients.*
>
> ***—Diamond (1991)***[10]

My opinion is the reliability of the different approaches to human evolution is fundamentally conditioned by the robustness of their respective assumptions. In DNA's case, the mechanisms which create and maintain genetic variability present many dark sides, such as the existence and effective relevance of those mechanisms which violate the classical rules of genetic transmission. As a further thought not lesser reason, the interpretations based on DNA data control but benefit from the verification and integration with knowledge derived from other, even the most traditional techniques. In fact, the use of differentiated methodologies offers the opportunity to examine the reliability of the assumptions behind each approach, and to probe in greater depth the significance of the different levels of biological variation. At the same time, by comparing the interpretations, which derive from the analysis of different biological aspects, it is possible to integrate not only different, but often complementary information: giving evolutionary reconstructions a greater completeness, one gives them greater reliability.

To answer many of the still open questions, it is therefore essential for anthropology to reaffirm its nature as synthetic discipline, capable both of approaching the complexity of human evolution by bridging different areas of research, and favouring the reciprocal "fertilization" between innovative and consolidated methodologies.

In this review, both specialistic[11] and divulgative[12] topics are dealt with and developed.

REFERENCES

1. Nuttall, G.F.H., *Blood immunity and blood relationship*, University Press, Cambridge, 1904.
2. Jacob, F. *Evoluzione e Bricolage. Gli "espedienti" della selezione naturale*, Einaudi, Torino, 1978.
3. Spedini, G. *Esistono le razze? dal concetto tipologico al nominalismo*. Anicia, Roma, in corso di stampa.
4. Manzi, G., Grimaldi, S., Destro Bisol, G. 'Fossil genetic and archaeological evidence of modern human origin/s: state of the art', in *Rivista di Anthropologia*, 1994, 72, pp. 243-69.
5. Stoneking, M. 'In defence of "Eve"—a response to Templeton's critique', in *American Anthropologist*, 1994, 96, pp. 131-41.
6. Hagelberg, E., Clegg, J.B. 'Genetic polymorphisms in prehistoric Pacific islanders determined by analysis of ancient bone DNA', in *Proceedings of the Royal Society of London*, 1993, 252, pp. 163-70.
7. Ross, E. 'Eloquent Remains', in *Scientific American*, 1992, 267, pp. 115-25.
8. Piazza, A., Cappello, N., Olivetti, E., Rendine, S. 'A genetic history of Italy', in *Annals of Human Genetics*, 52, 1988, pp. 203-13.
9. Ammermann, A.J., Cavalli-Sforza, L.L. *La transizione Neolitica e la genetica di popolazioni in Europa*, Boringhieri, Torino 1986.
10. Diamond, J.M. 'A way to world knowledge', in *Nature*, 1991, 352, p. 567.
11. Destro-Bisol, G. 'Migration, genetic variation and DNA polymorphisms', in *Current Anthropology*, 1993, 34, pp. 765-75.
12. Destro-Bisol, G. Manzi, G. 'Origini di una specie', in *Prometeo*, 1995, 13, pp. 102-10.

10

Human Development and World Peace

Shashi B. Sahai

Peace has been a cherished goal of man, who has been ravaged and scarred by unrelenting cycles of warfare all through recorded history. Buddha and Christ represented this universal human craving in their *avatar* as the most illustrious apostles of compassion for humankind, non-violence and peace. The first of the "Ten Precepts" or commandments which a person was to swear by while being initiated into the Buddhist order reads: "I accept the precept to refrain from harming living beings. The celebrated exortations of St. Paul on the virtue of charity echo somewhat similar sentiments: "Just as a mother, as long as she lives, cares for her only child, so should a man feel all embracing love to all living beings. He should feel boundless love for all the world above and across, unrestrained without enmity."

And yet, for Buddha and Christ and millions of their followers through the ages, peace, that is abnegation of war in the affairs of man has long remained a distant ideal, ever cherished but perceived as unattainable. History has been wallowing in oceans of blood through centuries. The first recorded history is an account of the protracted wars fought by the Greeks against the invading Persians and the recorder—Herodotus is acknowledged as the first historian of the world. Even some of the famous epics of prehistoric times which constitute the source material for construction of ancient history or proto-history are tales of one deadly war or another. The *Mahabharata*, the longest poetic work in the world, is all about a devastating war between Kauravas and Pandavas at Kurukshetra, the famous Greek epic *Illiad* is the story of the seige of Troy by Greek Kings and chieftains to recover the captured Greek beauty Helen.

Of all the ancient civilizations that flourished in Egypt, Mesopotamia, Hwang Ho valley in China, Indus valley in India, and Greece, the last is most well known because we have the record of its perennial wars and conquests. As Arnold Toynbee observes, the early marriage of war with Hellenic history, made war an integral feature of Hellenic life. An early fifth century B.C. philosopher—Aeracleitus of Ephesusi—almost defined the cult of war which he summed up as: "War is the father of all things".[1] The close linkage of war with Hellenic or ancient Greek–Roman civilization is significant because the modern western civilization owes its origin to that.

The known history of ancient medieval and modern world is a ceaseless chain of wars in pursuit of tribal, dynastic, religious and nationalist goals. From around mid-sixth century B.C. till the first quarter of fourth century B.C., the known or active world comprising West Asia, North Africa and southern Europe was rocked by a series of wars between the empire-builders of Persia—contemporaries of the Hellenes—and the Greeks culminating in the subjugation of the Persian empire by Alexander the Great. In the course of time the Greeks were superseded by the Romans in the Hellenistic world in Europe. This was followed by some of the most destructive wars of the ancient world beginning 264 B.C. between the Romans and the Carthaginians, holding sway over North Africa, spread well over a hundred years. The Punic wars as they are known, ended in the decisive defeat of the Carthaginians by the Romans in 146 B.C. paving the way for complete Roman domination of the most active part of the world for centuries.

The history of Rome is a record of unceasing wars of conquests which extended the sway of the empire at its peak to Italy, Spain and Gaul (France) in the West, Greece and Asia Minor in the East, Carthage and some other parts of the Mediterranean countries and Egypt in North Africa (a protected state). But the logic of war caught up with the Romans in due course and they were destroyed by warring tribes from northern Europe termed as "barbarians"—Goths, Franks, Visigoths, Vandals—by the last quarter of the fifth century A.D.

And then the advent of Islam in the sixth century A.D. led to the emergence of the desert people of Arabia as a fresh set of world conquerors inspired by extraordinary religious fervour. Armed with their new-found faith—Islam—the Arabs unleashed relentless wars subjugating the whole of Asia Minor and marched right up to Sindh in India (now in Pakistan). In the west, they easily conquered Egypt and went right across Northern Africa reaching the Atlantic ocean on the western coast of Morocco. From there they crossed the narrow sea into Spain and Europe. After conquering Spain rapidly the Arabs advanced into southern France where they were defeated at the battle of Tours in 732 A.D. In central Asia, they marched right up to the borders of Mongolia. The latent conflict between two highly proselytizing religious—Christianity and Islam—burst forth into religious wars known as "Crusades" towards the close of the eleventh century A.D. and rocked Europe and Asia for more than 150 years.

The subsequent history of the world is, if anything, even more war-scarred and blood-stained. The Mongol tribes led by Chengiz Khan, dubbed by Persian and Arab historians as the "scourge of god" and his successors ravaged the world for the best part of the thirteenth century. They were followed by another sturdy tribe from the steppes of Turkestan in Central Asia who took to the sword. Known as Ottoman Turks, they took up the cause of Islam and started a fresh series of religious wars which devastated the world from the fourteenth to around the first half of the sixteenth century.

There was what may be termed as a 'lucid interval' during the next two centuries when the dominant European countries indulged in relatively 'soft' dynastic wars to maintain some kind of a 'balance of power'. But the rise of Napolean in the wake of the French Revolution inaugurated the era of nationalist wars beginning the nineteenth century culminating in the two mega wars of the twentieth century. As Arnold Toynbee observes, "The fundamental reason why war was less atrocious in the eighteenth century than either before or since was that it had ceased to be a weapon of religious fanaticism and had not yet become an instrument of nationalist fanaticism".[2]

A cursory glance through history would thus suggests that right from the sacking of Knossos in the Augean Basin by the Greek Aryans towards the close of fifteenth century B.C. or later, down to our own times, every page of human history is soaked in blood. In 1960, a Norwegian statistician gave out that "in 5560 years of recorded human history there have been 14,531 wars" and that "of 185 generations of man's recorded experience only ten have known unsullied peace".[3] And as one writer has put it, recourse to war appears to follow no particular pattern in terms of race, form of governments, social order, or stage of development after the appearance of warfare some five thousand years ago".[4]

A View from Prehistory

The almost indelible imprint of history, or recorded history, on human psyche is that war is a historical necessity, an integral attribute of humanity. A view from prehistory would, however, reveal that the imprint is not really the product of human activities as such but of the records of activities left to us. It is the record-keepers, or historians, who have turned the history of man into a history of wars. A comprehension of the timeframe encompassing the evolution of our kind of humans—the *Homo sapiens* would set the records straight.

The earliest 'hominid' or 'homo' that is bipedal or two-legged apes with a brain—were around in East Africa over two million years ago. By around one and a half million years ago they developed into *Homo erectus* with a little larger brain and taller in size. It was around half a million years ago that *Homo erectus* evolved into *Homo sapiens*, that is the original modern human that spread across the world. Walking was, it seems, quite literally the first step on the road to being human; the big brain that we are so proud of, came later, perhaps because of the opportunities provided by upright walking to free the hands for complex tasks (such as tool-making) that needed a good brain."[5]

Fully modern humans, *Homo sapiens sapiens* also made their appearance around by 100,000 years ago, more or less at the beginning of the latest Ice Age in the present ice epoch. This is backed by the discovery of part of a human skull, 1,15,000 years old, in a cave in South Africa.[6] And cave paintings from 40,000 years ago show a world of sophisticated European hunters and the animals they hunted, a grave site near present day Moscow more than 30,000 years old reveals traces of tailored clothing, including trousers, moccasin-type shoes, jackets and hats, all decorated with beads.[7]

With such a long past, how old is our history? By all accounts our history, or recorded history is not older than about 5,000 years. There was no history when our ancestors in the shape of two-legged apes with a brain appeared in Africa over two million years ago. There was no history when they developed into *Homo sapiens* around half a million years ago. There was no history when they further evolved into fully modern humans with a bigger brain—the *Homo sapiens* about 1,00,000 years ago and indulged in cave paintings some 40,000 years ago. They lived in peace (or rather without war) for millennia, feeding upon nuts, roots, insects and whatever came their way. Even when they got organized into groups and tribes they went about gathering roots and fruits and hunting animals for food without one group coming in contact with another necessitating a clash. The earliest *Homo sapiens sapiens*—that is, our own human species—existed in the world around a hundred thousand years ago, but the history of war is only around 5,000 years old. That would indicate that man has lived twenty times more in peace than in war. Only a holistic view of our past from across the frontiers of history can restore the perspective and obliterate the impress of war as a historical inevitability from human psyche.

Social Evolution of Man

Once the deadweight of history on our consciousness is removed, it becomes easier to see how human society has evolved through and towards peace and survival rather than war and death. Even post-Darwinian socio-biologists insist than man has survived and multiplied because of "reciprocal altruism" because he has been able to reason compromize and cooperate with his kind. He is an "altruistic ape" with altruistic instincts and ability to reason and compromize being coded, directly or indirectly, in his DNA. His self-interest in most cases is enlightened self-interests, which is the bedrock of inter-personal, inter-social and international relationships. As one writer has put it, "if hamadryas baboons had nuclear weapons, they would destroy the world in a week".[8] But humanity has lived with nuclear weapons for five decades because he is endowed with that "superior logic" or intelligence which, in biological terms, separates him from the ape.

Man's ability to cooperate and accommodate, stemming from "reciprocal altruism" rooted in his DNA according to modern socio-biologists, contributed his social living in a complex society of "reciprocal altruists". This led to the evolution of institutions of family, tribe, kingdom and nation—state in due course of time. All these institutions were basically utilitarian catering to some basic needs of man and contributing to his betterment in given situation. As the primitive man inched forward from immediate family to living in groups or herds, need arose for a certain amount of regulation of the behaviour of members of the group. When they stumbled upon food producing and animal rearing, it lead to agriculture and settled life and some rudimentary rules or codes enforceable by the community as a whole emerged to make community living possible. That was the genesis of the institution of tribe, the earliest social collectivity in human history to command loyalty of the individual.

To start with, regulatory decisions binding on the members were taken by the community as a whole. Gradually, every tribe started have a leader or chieftain, perhaps chosen for his quality of leadership to facilitate the working of the system as the numbers increased. Over a period of time, many tribal chieftains became kings. The Central Asian tribes which came to China and founded the Hwang Ho civilization around 4000 years ago, had their chiefs or patriarchs elected by the members of their tribes. A couple of centuries later, one of them named Yao started calling himself an emperor. Yet he was not succeeded by his son, but nominated another member to succeed him. It was only later, that the title became hereditary laying the foundation of the first Chinese dynasty known as the Xia dynasty. Dynasticism thus grew out of tribalism in the social evolutionary process and kings started commanding total loyalty of individuals living in their kingdoms.

From kingdom to modern nation state was but a short step in terms of man's long past, though it took centuries to evolve in terms of history. A republican state system developed fairly early in the city states of ancient Greece. (Rome also started as a city state though it grew into a kingdom or empire subsequently.) But it was not until the sixteenth century that nationalism or nation state started emerging as the all powerful socio-political institution in Europe. It was initially enveloped in the veil of dynastic monarchy and had to wait until the French Revolution to come to its own. It was only after the deadly blow inflicted upon the institution of monarchy as such in course of the French Revolution that republican nationalism emerged as the most powerful institution of human society.

And like the institutions of tribe and kingship earlier, the nation-state was also a product of necessity. In sixteenth century Europe a complex set of factors like vast geographical discoveries and ever expanding trade and commerce created a situation which could be best taken care of by the nation-state. Tremendous economic opportunities opened up by the discovery of the New World and sea routes to the East beckoned to be exploited. The emerging commercial class looked up to the nation-state for support in face of restrictive particularities at home and competition abroad. The peoples of Europe, aroused by 'Renaissance' to a healthy this worldliness and inspired by Enlightenment in pursuit of material well-being, needed an authentic political instrument to enable them to avail of the new economic opportunities. The nation-state admiringly filled the bill.

But all these need-based utilitarian human institutions—tribe, kingdom and nation-state—have in their own time been compulsive instruments of war. Somewhere in the process of their evolution, each of these institutions was mythified into something bigger than its worth, kind of a sacred cause calling for supreme sacrifice of human life itself. The migratory movements of the marauding tribesmen from the steppe land of Central Asia about 4000 years ago were probably the result of increase in numbers and need for new territories to accommodate them. But by the time their descendants—the Greek Aryans went about destroying Knossos in Crete and conquering territory right up to the Atlantic coast of North Africa, the myth of Hellenes, inborn right to rule over "lesser breeds" had become the prime motivating force behind their unceasing wars. Similarly, myths and legends grew around kings and emperors accounting for innumerable dynastic wars of ancient and medieval times. And finally, the advent of nationalism inaugurated the era of nationalist wars culminating in the most devastating mega wars of the twentieth century. It is the alchemy of myth which in course of time raised these need-based institutions to the status of cult in promotion of which endless wars have been fought through the ages.

Once an institution is mythified into a cult, the commitment of its members to it is much more than in proportion to the benefits tangible or intangible accruing from it. If the benefits are quantified and measured as 10, the gratification that the success of a cult brings to its adherents can be 100 or 1000 or more. All the great wars of history have been fought in pursuit and promotion of one cult or the other—the tribal, dynastic, religious and nationalist. But each of these cults has in due course spent itself up bringing an end to its own kind of war. The Mongol wars were the last of the tribal wars, the Ottoman Turk wars the last of the religious wars, the Thirty years' war the last of the dynastic wars (between Hapsburgs and Bourbons) and the Second World War the last of the great nationalist wars of history. The great war or world war regime would have ended in 1945 but for the eruption of another cult of war par excellence—Marxism on the world scene. With the end of Marxism as a cult in its own heartland, humanity has entered the stage of a warless existence. At long last, mankind has steered clear of the aberrant course of perennial warfare in sight of its true destiny—pursuit of happiness in peace. The "altruistic ape" seems to be coming to its form.

New Economism

The cardinal factor which has brought this about is: greater free play of man's innate urge for pursuit of earthy human gratifications. Conceptually, it may be close to the Freudian 'pleasure principle' in consort with the 'reality principle' which constitutes the human instinctual structures. In more commonplace terms, it may be described as new economism or even consumerism in a very broad sense. Material well-being has always been a very important concern of man, as promoter of happiness, but not always the primary concern. In olden times, there was not much more to material well-being than gratification of basic physical needs of food, shelter and carnal instincts. Nothing much extra by way of physical or mental satisfaction was either available or conceived of. And saturation level of conceivable basic needs was low and static. All that has drastically and dramatically changed now.

At the physical plane, so much has been created and is being multiplied so fast to add to the pleasures of living. The range and sweep of material goods and services, which make life worth living available today and people's ever growing craving for them is fast eroding the sway of myths and cults as promoters of war. People would much rather live with them than die for a cause, however sacred it might have been for their ancestors. The over-riding concern of men in all societies is to better their material well-being. Higher and still higher standards of living, entailing full enjoyment of benefits of modern civilization, is the prime objective and principal aspiration of peoples in developed as well as developing countries. There is no space available in the human mind today to entertain any cult or 'ism' worth dying for. Such mega 'isms' as nationalism which plunged the world into history's most destructive wars and Marxism which threatened to do so, are falling by the wayside in the process of man's evolutionary march. Marxism has evaporated in the land of its glory and nationalism is evaporating in the land of its birth—western Europe —in the wake of man's zest for life and pursuit of pleasure in peace.

And material satisfaction, in the narrow sense of physical comfort or enjoyment is not the only component of human pleasure. A more important ingredient of human gratification is mental pleasure derived from enjoyment of beauty and pursuit of knowledge. Aesthetic and intellectual gratifications are more pleasurable and durable than any physical gratification. There may be a limit to sensory satisfactions of human body, but there is no limit to the cravings and satisfactions of human mind. Knowledge in fact is pleasure, which we as humans are privileged to enjoy by virtue of one per cent difference in our DNA from that of the pygmy chimpanzee (we are 99 per cent ape in our genetic material, but the one per cent difference has made all the difference). With its ever-widening horizon, ranging from the minutest world of atom to celestial space, knowledge has broken all boundaries of mental pleasure, making it a limitless source of joy. It is an index of the growing importance of mental pleasures in the hierarchy of human satisfactions that media and entertainment constitute the single largest industry in the biggest industrial country of the world—the United States of America.

Peace for All Time

The inexorable thrust of human development is therefore towards peace. Man's instinctive structure and intellectual endowment are unmistakably leading humanity to a war free world. If we are not able to recognize the obvious, it is because of the deadweight of five thousand years of history on our thinking process. In our long past, aberrations like cannibalism, head-hunting and incest had their sway, but each of these withered away in due course. An aberration like slavery continued in human society right up to the Modern Age in our recent past, but this also was wiped out in course of social evolution. If the scourge of war is similarly blotted out from the world, it will only be a minor event in the evolutionary stride of human society. Hopefully, to the future generations two hundred years from now, war may appear as much of a barbaric anachronism as slavery or head-hunting appears to us today.

The only caveat that has to be entered here is that the advent of a warless world does not mean the end of all quarrels and conflicts between and among diverse human collectivities. These are in the nature of human family disputes and international law and order problems which can be taken care of by the evolving institutional framework of international relations. It only means the end of the protracted era extending over several millennia in which the most active segments of humanity fought great wars to conquer the known world or the world that mattered to them. The Central Asian tribes, the Greeks, Persians, Romans, Arabs, Mongols, Ottoman Turks down to the modern European nation states, all indulged in big wars to conquer the world that was worth conquering. It is that kind of great war or world war regime which has come to an end in the natural course of human development. In its unceasing evolutionary march, humanity has reached the important milestone of peace after a relatively long and painful journey.

REFERENCES

1. Quoted in, *Hellenism: The History of A Civilization*, by Arnold J. Toynbee.
2. *A Study of History*, by Arnold J. Toynbee.
3. Time Essay, *Time*, September 24, 1965, On War as a permanent condition quoted in *International relations* by Norma D. Palmers and Howard C. Perkins.
4. Charles Hodges, Why War? *Contemporary World Politics*, by F.J. Brown, Charles Hodges and J.S. Roucek, 1940.
5. Being Human by Mary and John Gribbin, 1993.
6. *Ibid*.
7. *Ibid*.
8. *On Human Nature* by Edward O. Wilson.

11

Forli

Historical Outline

Let us consider the name first: Forli. The classical origin of the place-name is apparent: Forum Livii (i.e. Livius' Forum). On the other hand, the city's date of origin and the mythical founder's identity are far less evident.

Scholars cannot reach an agreement on this matter. According to one hypothesis, the first centre of the forum was established at the beginning of the 2nd century B.C. (188 B.C., to be exact). Another suggestion has it that this city is certainly more recent by c.a. 150 years, as it was reportedly founded in Julius Caesar's days.

In any case, the identification of Marcus Livius Salinator, the consul who defeated Hannibal's brother, Hasdrubal, in 207 B.C. at the Metauro River, as the city founder is definitely unacceptable.

The founding father of the city can perhaps be found in Marcus' son, Caius Livius Salinator, mentioned twenty years later. These are, however, only presumptions; there is no reliable source. Another controversial matter revolves around the alternative name 'Figline'. The first to bring up the question was the distinguished physician Giambattista Morgagni who also carried out historical research and—in his work *Epistole Emiliane*—touched on archaeological, literary, and philological subjects with competence and insight that cannot but be admired even today. Morgagni had previously examined the so-called 'Libro Biscia', a parchment codex containing various—mainly longlease—contracts stipulated by the abbot of St. Mercurialis and other parties. The legal transactions spanned from 894 to 1398, thus providing us with valuable local information and historical data. On surveying the book, Morgagni noticed a recurring phrase in the first documents:

In hac civitate Liviensi que vocatur Figline (1092, translated as, "In this city of Livius which is called Figline"), or *In civitate Ficline que vocatur Liviensis* (1114, "In the city of Ficline which is called of Livius"). Morgagni's somewhat amazed comment was: "Although I can't say anything precise about the above names, there is no doubt that they meant Forli in those sentences".

In fact, the name Figline was common to other Italian places and was used to stress how important the potter's trade was locally. The surroundings did not lack kilnfiring raw materials such as clay, water and wood, and kiln remains have been discovered in different spots which, in Roman days, were found in the outer suburbs or in the open country.

These are, however, rare and isolated pieces of evidence, and no more mention was made of Figline after 1116.

Anyway, the debates and disputes concerning Forli's official date of birth cannot disregard the fact that the region had already been inhabited by local peoples as well as Celtic invaders—the Gauls, who had intermarried with the natives—since the 5th century B.C.

The whole of Romagna underwent a dramatic change when the Via Aemilia was planned and constructed following the Roman conquest, and Forum Livii was founded on the remains of Gallic villages.

In the following centuries, Forli enjoyed comparative peacefulness and no fame at all. For over five centuries, it must have functioned only as a collecting and distributing station for the farming produce of the surrounding, exceptionally fertile area.

Lying between the rivers Rabbi and Montone, it stood on a sort of island, its only worry being survival in case of floods, until —in the Middle Ages (1050)—the river system was regulated and water was diverted out of town. The logical interpretation of a few legends about the saints Mercurialis, Forli's patron, and Ruffillo, Forlimpopoli's patron, convey the idea of the first bishops working to reclaim the marshy, unhealthy terrain situated east of Forli along the course of the river Ronco. Situated on the well-travelled route of all the armies and peoples who invaded Italy, Forli is likely to have suffered brutality and destruction by Alaric and his Visigoths early in the 5th century A.D.

Alaric, in fact, is connected with a naive story which glorifies St. Mercurialis and explains the origin of the name of the most important and ancient borough of Forli, Schiavonia.

For another 800 years, up to the early 13th century, the city passively shared the same fate as the rest of Romagna, constantly subjected to the succeeding ruling peoples: Goths, Byzantines, Lombards and Franks.

The only notable fact on which both chroniclers and historians agree is that around the 10th century, perhaps as early as 889, Forli proclaimed itself a republic and responded to the Church's claims of temporal rule by overtly supporting the emperors of the Holy Roman Empire. Its loyalty made it known as the Ghibelline city par excellence and this fame outlived the following centuries.

Suddenly, Forli came to the forefront of 13th-century civil and religious struggles playing one of the main roles. In those days countless battles were fought against neighbouring Guelph cities, especially Faenza and Bologna. Two events deserve to be mentioned: in 1241, Forli loyally aided Emperor Frederick II to take Faenza and, as a token of the emperor's gratitude, the city was given permission to decorate its coat of arms with the Swabian eagle, which consequently pushed the older insignia—a white cross on a vermilion shield—into the background. Among the other privileges granted to the Forli city-state were the right of coinage and permission for its senators to wear ermine-lined purple robes.

However, fortune abandoned the House of Swabia after some twenty years and the emperor's most active and loyal lieutenant in Italy, Guido da Montefeltro, had to take shelter in Forli, the last Ghibelline stronghold, where he was asked to take on the office of Capitano del Popolo, i.e., commander of the local militia.

In this capacity, he led his army—which also included several refugees, exiles and bandits—from one victory to another. To mention just a few: the victories against Bologna (June 15th, 1275) near San Procolo bridge, situated between Florence in Civitella (November 14th, 1276); and, lastly, the most sensational feat, i.e. the Battle of Forli, on May Day, 1282. On that occasion, apart from his valour, the noble man from Montefeltro made his excellent tactics clear in an extremely bloody fight where the enemy was routed. This was the cream of the French army sent by Pope Martin IV to subjugate the rebel city in Romagna. With that deed, Forli earned a mention in a famous couplet of Dante's Inferno:

La terra che fe' già la lunga prova
e di Franceschi sanguinoso mucchio (Inf. XXVII, 43-44)

(This can broadly be translated by: The land that showed extraordinary endurance, and made a bloody heap out of the French army.)

Humiliation was intense for the French pope, who, one year later, organized a punitive expedition with the funds raised for a future crusade and replaced the defeated commander (the valiant, though unfortunate, Giovanni d' Appia) with Guido di Monforte. No battle was necessary, as the threats of retaliation against the exhausted population persuaded the Forli Senate to surrender unconditionally while Guido di Montefeltro, feeling betrayed, left the city with his followers.

Subsequent events brought about the expulsion of the papal legate, while the Ordelaffi family solved, in their favour, the question of supremacy with internal skirmishes. The Ordelaffis were to rule the city for almost two centuries.

Among the most remarkable members of this family, said to be of German origin, mention should be made of Scarpetta III, who gave Dante shelter when the great poet sojourned in Forli (1303), and Francis the Great, who fought against Egidio Albornoz, the cardinal leading an impressive army sent once again to subdue Romagna for the Papacy. Francis was defeated—on July 4th, 1359 —but historical records handed down the memory of his valour and that of his brave spouse, Marzia degli Ubaldini, to whom he had entrusted the defense of Cesena.

The best-known Ordelaffi, however, was Pino III, who firmly ruled Forli from 1466 to 1480.

Pino III was a man of his time in all respects: grandeur and baseness, cruelty and generosity marked his reign.

This is not the time to go into the family feuds and court conspiracies of those days. What should be pointed out here is that under Pino III the city was embellished with buildings and monuments and fortified through the finishing of the outside main walls and radical work carried out on Ravaldino Castle. The arts thrived, and Forli citizens lived in a time of 'enlightened peace' (although the inverted commas are compulsory here on various grounds).

When Pino died at the age of forty-four—hints of a possible poisoning were also dropped—the subsequent state of affairs plunged Forli into confusion: over the following few months, power lay in the hands of various members of the Ordelaffi family (Sinibaldo, Pino's natural son; the widow Lucrezia Pico; the nephews Antonio, Francesco and Ludovico). Sixtus IV, a 'nepotist' pope, claimed Forli for one of his relatives, who did not possess any outstanding quality apart from his papal kinship. Girolamo Riario's—this was his name—greatest merit was to be the husband of Caterina Sforza, whose name is related to the last historically remarkable events in Forli. Caterina married three times: Girolamo Riario, Jacopo Feo (a secret wedding, as the biographer Pier Desiderio Pasolini assures), and Giovanni de' Medici. The mother of a dozen children, she was the undisputed ruler of Forli and the appropriate successor to Pino Ordelaffi, even with reference to both her atrocities and excesses.

Nevertheless, her reign, too, was short as it was brutally overwhelmed by Cesare Borgia's plans of supremacy—a fate shared by several other minor feudal domains and towns in the Papal States (January 1500).

When Borgia's reign came to an abrupt end, the Ordelaffi family was back in power a short time (1503-1504) until Forli was annexed to the Papal States by express order of Pope Julius II (formerly Giuliano della Rovere); that was the actual end of Forli's independence.

Three centuries of obscurity ensued until civil feuds (between the Morattini and Numai families) brought about the establishment of the Court of the Ninety Peacemakers, a useful body meant to watch over public security.

Though Forli history slowly turned to a chronicle, we cannot fail to mention such significant events as the appearance of Giambattista Morgagni's genius (1682-1771); the vast collection of paintings by Carlo Cignani and his school (early 18th century); the restoration, renovation and building of palaces and churches under the supervision of Giuseppe Merenda, an architect who deserves mention even outside the limited city boundaries.

This long sort of lethargy was broken by the wave of innovation that the French Revolution has spread all over Europe. In June 1796, the Jacobin army entered Forli, while Napoleon made his triumphant entry into the town on February 4th, 1797, on the day that for centuries has been dedicated to the festivities in honour of Our Lady of the Fire, the city patron (we feel somehow that Napoleon did not choose that date purely by chance).

In spite of the French troops' plundering, looting and bullying, especially of noble families with large property and religious congregations, the populace got involved in the general excitement and a great number of Forli citizens served in Napoleon's army in the following years.

The days of the Kingdom of Italy, even though under French protection, shook up a population which had been subjugated for centuries and was by then completely unused to fighting in the name of grand ideas such as the Fatherland and Freedom. The result was that after Napoleon's decline the first lodges of the Carbonari and a number of conspirators made their appearance in Forli, too.

The Restoration returned Forli under the temporal power of the pope who opted for a sort of iron-hand rule by means of foreign or mercenary troops that treated the patriots with ferocity, so much so that Forli took active part in the 1831 revolts which were stifled with a bloodbath within one year.

Participation in the wars of independence and response to Giuseppe Garibaldi's generous appeals were also passionate (at least the name of Achille Cantoni, the young hero who fell at Mentana in 1867, should be mentioned here).

Most of the 19th century was predominated—in Forli—by the great personality of Aurelio Saffi (1819-1890). A strict follower of Mazzini, he played a main role in the exciting venture of the Roman Republic in 1849. An exile wanted by the Austrian police, he never lost touch with the Italian state of affairs and worked in every possible way for the unification of the country until the Kingdom of Italy was proclaimed.

He was a deputy (member of the Italian lower house), and his deep knowledge of economic and social matters allowed him to contribute significantly to the first acts performed by the national

Parliament. Everybody respected him as an upright, honest gentleman.

Although constantly pressed by those who wanted him to continue taking part in Parliament's political conflicts, Saffi decided to dedicate his last twenty years of life to study and teaching. During that period, he also held the modest (by his standard!) office of town councillor in Forli.

Forli citizens' participation in World War I was truly massive: a thousand or so of the hundreds of Forli volunteers shed their blood over the pits in Carso, the rough soil of Mount Grappa, and the waters of the Piave River.

In honour of them all, we will mention Fulceri Paulucci de' Calboli, in whose memory a gold medal for military valour was awarded.

Historians have perhaps not yet fully understood the significance that Benito Mussolini's activity in Forli had for local politics over the second decade of the 20th century. From here, he soared to the dictatorship which subjugated Italy for over twenty years.

The disastrous Fascist venture plunged Italy into all sorts of war up to its defeat in 1945. Forli suffered very heavy casualties, the civilian dead exceeding the number of the loss of remarkable monuments and works of art were the results of the bombing, retaliation, acts of oppression and violence by foreign troops and of the disorders caused by a bloody civil war.

Over forty years have now elapsed since those grievious days; Forli has grown rapidly and has over 100,000 inhabitants today. The city has been rebuilt completely and provided with all the services which a medium to large sized city cannot lack, let alone a provincial capital! Everything can be found here, apart from a theatre, but this is another story.

Basic Information

Geographical coordinates of the city:
Latitude: 44°13' N
Longitude: 12°03' E
City area: 228.1939 sq km
City altitude (Town Council): 34 m above sea-level

Highest point in the communal area (Ca' Brusa-Lardiano): 302 m above sea-level.

Lowest point in the communal area (Casemurate): 11 m above sea-level — Forli shares its boundaries with Faenza, Russi and Ravenna to the north; Ravenna, Bertinoro and Forlimpopoli to the east; Bertinoro, Meldola and Predappio to the south; Castrocaro and Terra del Sole to the west.

Resident population: 108,871 (1994 census)

No. of households: 42,142

Hydrography: The city lies between two rivers. Along the course of the Montone (to the west) the densely populated suburb of Cava has recently sprung up. To the east stands Ronco, formerly a small outlying district 4 km away from Forli which is now firmly included in the town's outskirts. Inside Ravenna province, both rivers flow together giving birth to the Fiumi Uniti (joined rivers).

Connections: The capital of the Forli province, the city has its railway station on the Bologna-Ancona railway line; in addition, it is served by local buses which connect it with all surrounding centres and seaside resorts on the Adriatic Coast.

Following are a few main distances:

Cesenatico, 34 km (by state roads)

Bellaria-Igea Marina, 42 km (by state roads)

Rimini, 49 km (by state roads)

Riccione, 60 km (by state roads)

Cattolica, 68 km (by state roads)

Ravenna, 27 km

Bologna, 63 km (by state road 9, Via Aemilia)

Florence, 109 km (by state road 67); 146 km (by the Al motorway via Bologna)

Milan, 281 km (by state road 9, Via Aemilia); 275 km (by the Al motorway).

Rome, 355 km (by state road 3, Flaminian Way); 347 (by state road 71 through Umbria and Casentino)

The Ridolfi Airport is situated in Via Seganti n. 103 - Tel. 0543/780049 and is served by domestic and international flights under the supervision of its air control. A bar and a restaurant can also be found there.

Economic Structure

Farming produce: Sugar - beets, vegetables, cereals, and fruit.

Several poultry-breeding farms have been established in and around Forli, and their output of poultry and eggs is considerable, so much so that Forli's market share in this field is considered among the largest in Italy.

Two thriving cooperative wine-grower's associations collect quality grapes from their associates to make wines which are exported to and appreciated in all countries.

Handicraft: Decorative art (ceramics and graffito work); a craftwork school and an embroidery vocational school; several medium-sized factories.

An Itinerary of the City

Reaching its peak of expansion at the end of the medieval period under the rule of the Ordelaffi family, Forli has, in what are described today as its 'historic boroughs', maintained its urban character. This character remained unaltered until the beginning of the 20th century when walls were knocked down in order to facilitate the continuous expansion of the city. This expansion, as we can see today, stretches as far as the residential suburbs of Ronco.

However, the traditional boroughs, 'Borghi', have retained their old names, and these boroughs will be explored in our artistic itinerary of the town.

Forli is, relatively speaking, a small town; and with a carefully planned itinerary even the most exacting tourists will be able to visit and sightsee all the places of interest in the space of one day.

Let's begin from what, in all senses of the world (artistic, cultural, economic and religious), is considered the heart of Forli; Saffi Square (Piazza Saffi).

For centuries, Piazza Saffi was called Piazza Maggiore (the largest square), and prior to that, when the old Foro Romano (Roman Forum) stretched as far as what is today the portico of the Town Hall, it was named Campo dell' abate (Abbot's Field), derived from the St. Mercurialis church where the Vallombrosian monks resided.

The building which runs along one side of the square and

faces towards the east is the seat of the Town Council. The present style is that of the 18th century and was probably determined by Cardinal Stanislao Sanseverino (1764-1826), although the original construction may perhaps be accredited to Cardinal Legate Egidio Al-bornoz, notwithstanding certain modifications which were made by the Ordelaffi and Riario families.

Next to the Town Council, in the part of town which today is still called Rialto Piazza, lies the Palazzo del Podestà. The building's precise year of construction has been dated by historians as between 1459 and 1460. Despite having undergone much reconstruction during this century, the building's sombre and severe style does not remain unnoticed. Adjacent to Palazzo del Podestà is Albertini Palace; elegant yet airy, this building openly displays its Renaissance style. The building is now at the citizens' disposal and its rooms are used for displaying town projects or events such as art exhibitions and different types of expositions. Debates and conferences are held on the ground floor.

The third building, facing towards the south, is the Palazzo del Credito Romagnolo. Its present style was determined by the Forli architect Giuseppe Missirini, however, in 1926, a final adjustment was made to the corner verging with Via Volturno.

On the east side of the square, the Chamber of Commerce and Telecommunications Office apart, you can see what is considered to be the crowning glory of Forli architecture: the Basilica of St. Mercurialis. In 1980, the town celebrated the 800th anniversary of the construction of the belfry.

The church's portal displays a series of carvings depicting the 'Dream and Adoration of the Three Kings', by the same artist who painted 'The Months' in Ferrara's cathedral (13th century). Inside the church you can admire paintings, recently relieved of the baroque superstructures and adornments which had nothing in common with the paintings' original austerity. You can admire paintings by Cignani, Palmezzano, Carrari and other notable local artists.

Entering the church, you can see on the right-hand side the sarcophagus of Barbara Manfredi, which is one of Francesco di Simone Ferrucci da Fiesole's masterpieces. The sarcophagus was transferred to St. Mercurialis from St. Jerome after the latter was heavily bombed by the Germans in 1944. The sculpture, which was in an advanced state of decay, finally underwent very serious restoration work. The lovely 15th-century cloister next to the basilica, to which the public had access during the Fascist regime, is now both disfigured and spoilt, as is the well which is in its middle. The fact that it could be used by the general public as a means of crossing from one square to the other seems to have stripped it of all its fascination and aesthetic, cultural appeal.

The fourth side of the square is taken up by the Post and Telegramme Offices, designed by Cesare Bazzani and built in 1932. Other historical buildings had to be demolished before erecting the new edifice. The destruction, in particular that of the Casa Castellini Pantoli, was an extremely painful process.

Rialto Piazza is the ideal starting point for a tour of the town's most interesting sites. From here, we stroll through the old borough Schiavonia, now named Corso Garibaldi. Shortly after passing Giorgina Saffi Street, we can admire the splendid 16th-century Pawnbroker Palace which lies on our left and is now the seat of the Italian Automobile Association. Taking the first turn on the left, after several hundred metres you will come to the Oratorio di San Sebastiano (15th century), designed by the architect Pace Bombace. Nearby rises the imposing edifice of St. Dominic, which has been reduced to a precarious state through the ravages of time and carelessness of man. The building's interior will constitute the site for the new Town Theatre.

It was perhaps the most famous and richest amongst the churches in Forli due to its marble and works of art, but on account of a series of mishaps, starting with the suppression of religious orders in 1866, it is now in very bad condition.

Having walked back to Corso Garibaldi, following the road as far as the first big bend, you come across the large Piazza degli Ordelaffi (Ordelaffi Square). The Paulucci Piazza Palace is situated at the far end of the square. This palace was built at the end of the 17th century along the lines of the Lateran Palace in Rome. Left unfinished for over two centuries, it was finally completed at the beginning of the 20th century. Today it is the seat of the Prefecture and also contains the apartments of the Civil Governor.

In the middle of the square stands the Cathedral, which over a millennium of years underwent so many architectural changes that the original structure is now no longer recognizable. The last readjustment, completed in the middle of the 19th century, was to render the facade similar to the style of the Patheon.

Inside the cathedral many precious works of art have been preserved, and one which merits particular attention is the fresco on the ceiling of the dome of Our Lady of the Fire's Chapel, which depicts the Assumption. The fresco was painted by Carlo Cignani over a period of 25 years and was, from both a technical and artistic point of view, an extremely time-consuming and difficult work of art. Another notable work of art is the large Romanesque crucifix at the end of the left-hand aisle. At the end of the right-hand aisle you can admire the beautiful baptismal fount sculptured by Tommaso Fiamberti and Giovanni Ricci. Paintings by Niccolò Rondinelli, Marco Palmezzano, Guido Cagnacci, and frescoes by Pompeo Randi all contribute to the cathedral's artistic wealth, adding warmth to the immense and solemn interior which has three irregular aisles divided by two rows of Corinthian columns.

Continuing along Corso Garibaldi, you can see Albicini Palace (containing paintings by Cignani), and Guarini Palace, which is renowned for its famous Renaissance-style courtyards. Opposite this stands the 15th-century so-called Palmezzano's House, in that it was owned by the celebrated Forli painter, although it appears that, contrary to popular belief, he never actually lived there.

In the adjacent street called Via Cesare Albicini stands the graceful Church of St. Joseph, which, if one should be lucky enough to find open, certainly merits a visit. The church belonged to the old Guild of Carpenters and has for its altar-piece a painting of its patron saint painted by Guido Cagnacci. In front of the church stands the house which was the birthplace of Aurelio Saffi. Today, it is the seat of the Historical Institute of the Resistance.

Once again, walking towards the old borough named Schiavonia, we can note on our right the 18th-century Gaddi Palace which today is owned by the Council and houses three museums: the Ethnographic Museum of Peasant Culture, the Museum of Risorgimento, and the Romagna Museum of the Theatre.

At the second bend in Corso Garibaldi, preceded by a small

square, stands the Church of the Holy Trinity. The church was restructured on already existing structures towards the end of the 18th century. It was in this part of the town, around the old church, that the town's nucleus was born. Inside the church, among other things, is Domenico Manzoni's funeral monument by Antonio Canova.

At the end of Corso Garibaldi, deprived of any important functions save that of a traffic roundabout, stands the only remaining, majestic Schiavonia Gate carried out in the 18th-century 'triumphal' style as desired by the Cardinal Legate.

So as not to confuse things, we ask our visitor to turn either left or right and walk back in the direction he came from, i.e. Rialto Piazza.

From here the city's second main street departs, which in 1928 was named after Armando Diaz. In the olden days, this borough was named 'Borgo dei Merloni' after one of the old families which resided there. However, very soon it became Borgo Ravaldino, as we are able to derive from reading Cardinal Angelico's 'Description' (1371). The new name originated from the hilly locality in the direction of which the old city gate of the same name, destroyed in 1874, was situated.

Corso Diaz has a winding course typical of medieval streets. This is probably also in part due to the fact that in days gone by the River Rabbi flowed through Piazza Saffi as far as the Town Council's archways. Today, the riverbed has had its course changed and now flows into the Montone River. The old riverbed is now a duct called 'Canale Ravaldino', the waters of which were for a long time used to power the watermills within the city walls.

A large part of the road surface was badly damaged when the Germans dropped one of their frighteningly powerful bombs on December 10th, 1944. In addition, private speculation and the building of huge modern edifices has altered the urban balance of what was once one of the most charming areas in this part of the city.

On the left, you will notice two splendid archways which are part of the Podesta Palace in Piazza Saffi, the baroque Orsi-Mangelli Palace, the solid Savorelli Prati Palace and, a little further on, the deconsecrated church Olde St. Anthony. This beautiful 12th-century construction, built in the Romanesque style and once used for a multiple of purposes (warehouse for cereals, dance hall, and hospital), has been restored and cleaned and is now a war memorial.

On the left still stands the church of St. Anthony the Abbot in Ravaldino, which is certainly worth visiting. The church, once home of the religious Carmelite order 'Brothers of the Porr', was designed by Carlo Cesare Scaletti. Adjustments were made by the Forli architect Giuseppe Merenda, who put his stamp on Forli's urban style in the 18th century. Inside the church some precious works of art have been conserved. Amongst these, there are at least two tableaux stemming from the 16th century: the Pieta by Livio Agresti and the Visitation by Marco Palmezzano.

At the end of the borough, preceded by a large square, stands the imposing Ravaldino Castle, opposite which there has been placed, with what one might call a distinct lack of aesthetic taste, the aqueduct's tower. This now rises above the Ravaldino Castle, also called Caterina Sforza's Castle, after the last and most illustrious tenant evicted—under cannonfire! —by Cesre Borgia on January 12th, 1500, after sixteen days of combat. Despite having undergone enormous restoration work, the castle is not open to the public and may only be visited on request accompanied by a careful expert.

The near future foresees a project which will allow for the accommodation of Museum of Arms and the transfer of the Town's Archeological Museum within the fortress's vast rooms.

The third borough to visit is that named St. Peter.

This borough begins in Piazza Saffi on the corner of Via delle Torri and Corso Mazzini. The area was used to construct the grandiose block of the State Building.

Earlier, this area was for some mysterious reason called 'Cantone del Gallo' (The Cock's Corner), perhaps on account of an inn which once bore the cock as its sign. During the twenty years of Fascism, this borough underwent radical changes following the demolition of many of its existing buildings.

At the end of the short, first part of the road which at present borders on the shopping precinct, there was once a Roman bridge called St. Peter in Scotto, named after the nearby homonymic church which was probably the seat of and resting place for Scottish pilgrims on their way to Rome, and it is from this that the name St. Peter's borough, which includes all the area between the right-hand side of Corso Garibaldi and the left-hand side of Corso Mazzini, is derived. The architects of the Fascist regime, the Anglo-American bombings and, lastly, private speculation were to have a decisive effect on the borough's interior design. Nevertheless, we would still like to point out some buildings, churches and works of art which enable one to endure this stroll through the bombastic Fascist palaces and the modern-day blocks of concrete that have defaced the area.

Turning around the State Offices on your left, you will come across the only remaining medieval Numai Tower which almost fell prey to a whimsical work of restoration that would have turned it into a residential palace. Its last owner, Mrs. Giulia Pedriali, designated it as a Club for Aviators in memory of her husband, Mario Fabbri.

Turning into Via Pedriali, alongside of which are several gentile palaces, the most notable being Foschi Palace, you will come to Via Achille Cantoni, which—keeping to the right—leads you back to Corso Mazzini.

As you walk along Via Achille Cantoni, you will note a 16th century palace, on the front of which there is some ashlar-work. This work, a somewhat pale imitation of Ferrara's splendid Palace of Diamonds, named the street Diamante (Diamond) until such a time when it was dedicated to Giuseppe Garibaldi's dear friend and unfortunate here of the battle of Mentana (1867).

On reaching Corso Mazzini, walking in the direction of the city's outskirt, you will immediately notice the facade of the Carmine Church, the entrance to which displays an admirable marble portal by Marino Marco Cedrino and is in itself a small art exhibition. Once, prior to the last restoration, the portal adorned the entrance to the cathedral, after which it lay abandoned in a warehouse for a long period of time until—in 1915—it was reinstated with what one might call a commendable sense of propriety and pertinence, becoming the portal of the Carmine Church. Tradition has always sustained that the figures on the lunette represent the town's patrons and that the knight in the centre is either an Ordelaffi or otherwise the mythical figure of St. Valeriano.

The interior of the church, the origins of which are medieval, has been revived in the style of the 18th century using the designs of the ever-present monk Giuseppe Merenda. It is probably Forli's best example of the baroque style.

The events brought on first by the suppression of religious orders under Napoleon in 1797 and then by the birth of the Kingdom of Italy deprived the Carmelite monks of their Convent (now the adjacent Carabinieri barracks). Among other losses were several pieces of art, one of which was Marco Palmezzano's masterpiece 'The Annunciation'.

Going over the ring-road, following the road to Ravenna, and just after the railway bridge, you will come across 'St. Mary of the Flower' Church. The early 17th-century building demonstrates an abundance of frescoes painted by Gianfrancesco Modigliani (17th century) and Pompeo Randi (19th century).

On the left-hand side of Via Ravegnana, not far from the church, lies the Monumental Cemetery where all Forli's important citizens have been laid to rest. Here you can find sculptures by excellent artists worthy of the utmost consideration.

In St. Peter's borough you can also see St. Blaise Church in St. Jerome, now reconstructed on what were once the ruins of the former church destroyed in December 1944. The church has conserved the celebrated Immaculate Conception, accurately restored, by the famous Bolognese artist Guido Reni.

The starting point for a stroll through the last borough, Borgo Cotogni, is one which has traditionally had an inexplicable appeal and is called Trebbo di Mozzapie, which roughly corresponds to the parvis of the Church of Suffrages.

If ever there was a church attributed in no uncertain terms to Giuseppe Merenda, real protagonist of Forli's 18th-century architectural and urban rebirth, it was the Church of Suffrages. Already at the turn of the 1950s this attribution was put to discussion. *The Encyclopaedic Dictionary of Architecture and Town-Planning* (1969), edited by Paolo Portoghesi, states under the heading 'Merenda' in its fourth volume that the church was without doubt the work of the Forli monk. Yet, under the heading 'Soratini' in its sixth volume, we find the confirmation that the beautiful church was the opera of the Camaldolite monk Giovanni Antonio Soratini. In 1983, a scholar from Rimini was, on account of abundant documentary evidence and arguments, able to tip the balance in Soratini's favour.

Borgo Cotogni, the name of which is derived from the old Cotogneto town estate at the bottom of Corso della Repubblica, is the most recent of the boroughs. Formed during the medieval period, attaining its present style at the end of the 15th century, this borough does not contain noteworthy buildings, that is unless one ventures into the inner areas. If, for example, you take the small road on the right, Via Flavio Biondo, you come across a small square named after Forli's famous anatomist Giambattista Morgagni.

In topographic terms, this part of town belongs to the borough Ravaldino, but it is without doubt easier to get to the borough via Corso della Repubblica.

Morgagni's statue, which once stood in the huge courtyard of the adjacent Palace of Studies, formerly Mission Palace which now belongs to the Provincial Administration, now stands in the middle of the square.

The statue was transferred to a place which was open to the public during the commemoration of Morgagni in 1931.

The majestic Provincial Palace, which incorporates the graceful baroque church bearing the stamp of Merenda and is deemed as one of the most significant works of the 18th century, stands opposite one of Forli's best-loved churches: Santa Maria dei Servi, also called St. Peregrin by Forli citizens.

Over the last centuries, the church underwent various architectural changes; but, starting from its very portals, we have evidence testifying to the ancientness of the church's founding (c.a.1250).

Entering the church, you can observe the burial place of the Numais, a Renaissance work by Tommaso Fiamberti and Giovanni Ricci, as well as frescoes by some of Forli's artists amongst which there is probably also Livio Agresti, Renaissance-style choir-stalls and a splendid crucifix of the Giotto school. Recently, critics attributed this work to Giuliano da Rimini.

Coming out of the church, turning left, you come face to face with a construction of noteworthy dedication and significance, Morgagni Hospital; however, over the last decade, the hospital's services and functions have been transferred to Vecchiazzano (c.a. 3 km from the town centre). Of all the future projects for the abandoned hospital grounds, that which appears to have taken precedence is the possible construction of the University of Romagna.

Continuing to our left, down Via San Pellegrino Laziosi, we find ourselves back in Corso della Repubblica, and furthermore, right in front of the Church of St.Lucy (17th century). The facade's two niches display the statues of St. John the Apostole and St. Francis of Paola, sculptured by the Faentine Graziani brothers.

The two saints, and not St. Lucy who was chosen by the town's people, are in fact the church's two patrons.

Inside the church there are the statues of the four Evangelists by Giuseppe Trentanove, as well as paintings by talented local artists.

Unfortunately, we cannot spend much time on the description of the Palace of Cultural Institutes, which stands almost opposite the church, as such a description would take up more than an entire volume.

The palace, which is undisputedly one of Merenda's works, was the city hospital for about 200 years and is—architecturally speaking—of great value. In 1922, all the civic collections were transferred from the Mission Palace to this palace. The former then became the academic site of the lyceums and technical schools.

The library 'A. Saffi' contains many rare and precious books, some of which stem from the despoliation of the convents.

Following the death of Carlo Piancastelli (1938), a patron of the arts from Fusignano, the civic collection has been enriched with a patronage of autographs, manuscripts, rare books and objects of art.

The section which from both a quantitative and qualitative point of view has the most impact is that containing documentaries on everything regarding Romagna.

The Picture Gallery is also in the same building and contains paintings by celebrated artists (Beato Angelico, Antonio Canova,

Jacopo delle Masegne, Guido Cagnacci, Lorenzo di Credi, Lorenzo Costa, the brothers Antonio and Bernardo Rossellino, Francia, Guercino, and Carlo Cignani), as well as works by Romagna's major artists from every era. At this point we should draw attention to two important donations: one by Giuseppe Verzochi (70 major contemporary artists, as well as a personal interpretation on the subject of 'work'); the other made by Giuseppe Pedriali (many works by Flemish artists and—among other things—two stupendous landscapes of Romagna, attributed to Andrea Locatelli). Also portrayed is an oxen-cart by Fattori which surprises on account of its enormous proportions.

Taking advantage of his presence in the building, the visitor would profit from a visit to the Archaeological Museum. Despite its modest proportions, the museum contains pieces which could hold their own in any larger collection: an Ostrogothic fibula; a metal shield-plate (5th century B.C.); an Etruscan stele (7th century B.C.); an Aeneolithic mould for the casting of arrowheads.

Patient assembly has allowed for an interesting permanent exhibition, in the Ethnographic Museum, of the most important and most practised activities of craftsmen in Romagna, as well as depicting the daily life of the peasant family under patriarchal rule at the end of the 19th century.

If after having visited the Cultural Institutes you still have some time at your disposal, you might like to stroll towards Victory Square, which cannot help but impress with its inequivocable examples of what was once the concept of Mussolini's grandeur.

During the Fascist regime everything changed, and the Agricultural Research Station on the right was dedicated to Arnaldo Mussolini. The Aeronautical College (now seat of various primary schools, a teacher's training college, and classical lyceum) bore the name of Bruno Mussolini, and the magnificent Station Road was named after Benito Mussolini. The infant school and industrial college of technology, found halfway down Station Road, were named after Rosa Maltoni Mussolini and the Duce's brother Arnaldo, respectively. Obviously, today the street names have been changed, but all the area bearing the stamp of Cesare Bazzani (who during the city's urban restructuring in the 1920s took the lion's share), of Cesare Valle, and Arnaldo Fuzzi, has remained untouched to the extent that its magnificence was able to influence post-war construction. Adjacent, in front of the war memorial and adorned by a wrought-iron gate, are the 19th century public gardens with trees among which, much to the delight of the children who visit the park each day, a small zoo was established c.a 20 years ago.

The XIIIth International Congress of Prehistoric and Protohistoric Sciences was held at Forli, Italy during 8th to 14th September 1996. The participants of this Congress were from almost all countries of the world. The scientific session of the Congress was organised into 18 scientific sessions, 23 workshops, 18 poster sections and 21 posters of the workshop.

The 12 selected papers printed in this book are the selected papers of the scientific session of the XIIIth International Congress of Prehistoric and Protohistoric Sciences of which I was chairperson. The discussion part of the scientific session of these papers are not included here because I feel that those are not of the general interest. These papers are being published in the interest of scientific knowledge and also because these are rare research papers in which the scholars and students of prehistory Archeology-Anthropology have much interest.

In the state of the Union the words prehistoric and proto-historic sciences mean all the disciplines such as Archaeology, Anthropology, Geology, Animal and Vegetal Palentology, Ethnology, Folkore and Sociology which contribute to the development of knowledge in the field of Prehistory. This international body was founded on 28th May 1931 as the successor to the Congress Paleoethologique International (1864) and the Congress International Anthropologie et al Archeologie Prehistorique (1867) on 29th September 1955 this Congress became a member of the International Council for Philosophy and Humanistic Sciences (CIPSH) which is associated with UNESCO.

The first paper traces the Anthropological researches and its development in India.

Prof. Guido Barbujani in his paper has analysed that non-genetics and linguistic can be used as a research tool in reconstructing the past of the human being.

Prof. Giorgio Manzi states that toward the end of the Middle

Plaestocene, archaic humans, living in three continents (Asia, Africa and Europe) and both hemispheres, after a long evolutionary history were subjected to selective pressures which influenced their biology and culture.

Prof. Francesco Barone in his paper mentions that the theme of evolution seems to appeal once again to popular imagination today, still characterized by the aspects of fascination and heated debate it caused in the past century, during the decades following the Darwinian theory about the Origin of animal species. It probably holds an even greater fascination and interest now because today historical transformation no longer appears as a prerogative of humans on the basis of a belief dating back to ancient times but rather of life itself because as Darwin's contemporary argued "human derive from apes" and even from the inorganic universe: in this universe evolution is the motor, while thermodynamic balance is the death.

Prof. Jens Poulsen writes that in Denmark today much of the farming concentrates on the production of the famous Danish bacon and beer. It is interesting to look at the archeology of countries which have specialized in plough agriculture way back in history and prehistory.

Prof. Luiz Oosterbeck presents an outline of the Origins, present and foreseen future of archeology at the Escola superior de Technologia de Tomar. The school has existed for only a decade and archeology has been taught for no more than six years. In 1983, though, a research programme on the transition to the agro-pastaralist economic model was set up by L Oosterback, A na R. Cruz and Carlo Martins.

Prof. Giancarlo Susini, in his paper prehistory and history, writes that, if history is regulated by time, it does not seem possible or at least it is arguable that there could be time outside history. We all know that in our everyday life time spent in waiting rooms is usually difficult to measure, so much so that the moment in which the waiting ends is conditioned by the psychosis created by the waiting. When the mind turns to prehistory, a large part of public opinion suffers from similar feelings to those felt by a patient in a waiting room: prehistory is almost universally considered as the waiting room of the history.

Prof. Emmannel Avati in his paper mentions that the first intellectual expressions of humankind lead us back to times immemorial. The discovery of our roots raises profound questions that affect the very identity of our species. In some prehistoric sites it has been noticed that homonids used to collect, transport and store stones and animal bones with partienlac shapes or colours, already during the lower paleolithic period. It is not easy to decide whether this attitude towards collecting should be regarded as an indication of certain intellectual capacities. In order to do this, it would be useful to understand the aims and the purposes of such behaviours.

Prof. Giovanni DestroBisol presents a short overview on the use of proteins and DNA as a tool for reconstructing human evolutionary history. After a discussion on some limitations of anthropometric characters for the anthropological applications, the concept of genetic polymerphism is explained. The relation between the development of Anthropological genetics and the failure of the concept of race in the second half of this century is then briefly reviewed.

Mr. S.B. Sahai has given an interesting scientific account of the Human Development and World Peace.

Dr. A.K. Singh, based on his empirical data, writes about secularism in the Indian context in terms of peace and religion.

Prof. Indira Prasad also presented her viewpoint on secularism in terms of the Indian context.

Index